ACADEMIC Success

HOLLY J. SEIRUP

Kendall Hunt
publishing company

CONTENTS

CHAPTER 1

Academic Success: Taking the First Steps

HOLLY J. SEIRUP

"Always bear in mind that your own resolution to succeed is more important than any one thing."
—*Abraham Lincoln*

WHAT IS ACADEMIC SUCCESS?

Each student defines academic success with different parameters based upon his or her own individual goals, dreams, and aspirations. Ultimately, having success academically means reaching your full potential by challenging yourself both in and out of the classroom. Successful students are able to define their academic goals, are motivated, and have multiple strategies to reach those goals. This book will be outlining various strategies and techniques to assist students reach their goal of academic success!

According the Bureau of Labor Statistics (2012), 68.3 percent of high school graduates in 2011 went on to college with six out of 10 attending a four-year institution. When asked why they went on to pursue higher education, the answers were quite interesting. They included:

- To continue my education
- To get a better job
- To please my family and friends
- I didn't know what else to do
- It seemed like the next step

Consider for a moment, what are your reason(s) for going to college? Please complete the following short exercise.

> The reason(s) I decided to attend college . . .

Setting Goals

To begin, it is important to assess and identify your individual goals for your college experience and why those goals are important to you. Goals can assist a person by providing direction, something for which to strive. Goal-setting can provide a map or a plan to get you from where you are to where you want to be. It can alleviate a feeling of floundering, being "lost," or having no direction. Here are some things to consider:

- Do you have specific learning objectives?
- Do you want to grow and develop personally as well as professionally?
- Are there vocational skills you want to master to get your "dream" job?
- Do you have a specific grade point average that you feel you need/want to attain?
- Is there an internship for which you aspire?
- Do you have co-curricular (leadership) goals?

Keep in mind while identifying goals that those that are most effective are realistic, measurable, and attainable. For example, grades are important and can impact one's ability to apply for some internships, leadership positions, and student teaching opportunities. Yet setting a goal to raise your GPA from a 2.0 to a 4.0 in one semester may be unrealistic. On the other hand, having a long-term goal to raise your GPA to over a 3.0 with a short-term goal to raise your GPA from 2.0 to 2.5 in one semester may be realistic, measurable, and attainable, particularly when implementing strategies to attain your goal. It is also important to be honest with yourself when considering goals. Being aware of your likes and dislikes, strengths and weaknesses, can enhance the goal-setting process and increase the probability of success. Ongoing self-awareness and self-assessment assist in the development of goals as well as help in the discovery of your academic passion which may also impact overall success.

It is important to begin by identifying your long-term goals which can be attained and supported by short-term goals.

Examples of long-term goals might be:

- Graduate from (name of college/university) by (date)
- Learn a new language by graduation
- Hold a leadership position on campus before senior year
- Get an internship during senior year
- Study abroad during junior year

After your long-term goals have been established, short-term goals can be identified to take steps to reach those goals. These may be for a semester or a specific year. Some examples of short-term goals might be:

- Raise my GPA by .5 point
- Research possible summer internships
- Apply to be a resident assistant

- Research study abroad opportunities
- Register for a Spanish class

Please reflect on your current goals and complete the following exercise.

My long-term goals (for college) are:

1.

2.

3.

My short-term goals (semester) are:

1.

2.

3.

Reaching Your Goals

Once you have identified your goals, the next step is developing a strategy/plan and identifying the support needed to reach the goals. For example, if the goal is to increase your GPA, consider what strategies you can implement to reach that goal. Begin by identifying the current academic strategies you are using, such as How many hours you study? Do you contact the professor if you have questions about course content? Do you attend class regularly? If your current strategies are working, and your goal is to increase your GPA, intensify the strategy by adding more time toward your academic pursuit. (There seems to be a correlation between time on task and success.) If you find that your current strategy is <u>not</u> working, such as you are not studying effectively, do not reach out to your professor when you have questions, and/or miss classes, then to reach your goal you would benefit from changing your strategy/plan. This might include:

- I will attend every class.
- I will be prepared to participate in class.
- I will attend a study skills workshop and practice new study strategies.
- I will identify additional hours to study for each class.
- I will meet with my professor at least twice during the semester.

Supporting Your Goals

Goals are sometimes difficult to reach and occasionally setbacks occur. If they do, it is a time to strengthen your resolve and motivation to achieve. It is imperative that one does not become discouraged and give up. Push forward—many great successes occur after we can appreciate what we learn from setbacks and challenges. Stay focused on your prior success and accomplishments and surround yourself with positive and supportive people. Many benefit from the support of others for encouragement and motivation to stay on track. You may have family members, friends, and other significant people in your life who play a supportive role in your goal attainment. Most colleges have also developed a strong support network for their students consisting of faculty, academic advisors, and mentors.

Academic Advisor   An academic advisor is often a crucial component of student success. The role of an academic advisor goes well beyond assisting a student with course selection and scheduling. An academic advisor is available to assist in all aspects of a students' academic life and serves as a resource regarding campus services. Advisors can be helpful with:

- Academic advice
- Assistance with personal and academic growth and development
- Registration and schedule planning
- Clarifying and answering questions about degree requirements and institutional policy
- Assistance with navigating the campus environment
- General information about campus life

Academic advisement is analogous with a partnership where both the advisor and the student are invested in the academic experience and success of the student. The advisor is available to support, encourage, and advise the student, and at the same time students are expected to take responsibility for their academic progress. Although other students may at times provide valuable information, do not rely on the "grapevine" when it comes to important academic information and deadlines. It is a good idea to meet with your academic advisor periodically throughout the semester so you can begin to build a supportive partnership. Advisors are a very valuable resource, and students are encouraged to meet with them regularly. Being prepared before an advisement meeting often enhances the outcome. The following are some helpful hints when meeting with your academic advisor.

- Bring a list of questions you may have regarding your major and university requirements.
- Discuss classes in which you are currently enrolled and those you are considering in the future.
- Ask for assistance if you anticipate difficulty with a course. Your advisor may be able to refer you to a tutor or writing or math learning centers.
- You may want to take notes at the meeting to review at a later time, or if a question regarding what you discussed arises.

Meeting with My Academic Advisor

Date_____

1. I am currently enrolled in:

2. Next semester, I am considering taking:

3. I am considering changing my major. Can you explain the implications?

4. When is the last day to withdraw from a course?

5. I am having difficulty with my biology class. Can I get a tutor?

6. Do I need a certain GPA before student teaching?

7. What is the policy about taking a course pass/fail?

8. Add your individual questions here . . .

Faculty   Faculty members are a tremendous resource to students both academically and as experts in their individual fields. Faculty office hours are usually posted on the course syllabus, in their department, and/or online. Students are encouraged to reach out to the faculty for academic advisement, if they have questions about class, and/or to discuss research interests or projects. Meeting with your faculty outside of class may provide additional intellectual enrichment and exploration. Faculty can provide guidance regarding educational opportunities that may maximize, enhance, and support students' academic experience and trajectory.

Other Mentors Many students are able to identify mentors on campus either within the faculty, alumni, or others administrative staff. Mentors serve as role models and often provide advisement, motivation, and support. They may be able to assist a student in clarifying his or her goals, further exploring careers, and providing professional networking opportunities and contacts.

TIPS: Some "Dos and Don'ts" of Academic Success

DO:

1. Schedule a reasonable course load: The average course load is 12–15 credits per semester, but consider other time commitments and responsibilities when scheduling.

2. Attend class: Missing a class in college can equate to missing an entire week of high school. Even with the very best intentions, it can be difficult to catch up. Also, check the syllabus for the professors' policy on absences. Missing class can impact your grade.

3. Prepare ahead: Come to class having completed the readings and with questions you may have. Find a seat in the classroom where you will not be distracted and can focus on listening to the professor and learning the material presented.

4. Read the syllabus: There is a great deal of information and policy in each syllabus. You will be responsible for the assignments and readings outlined. If you have any questions, contact your professor.

5. Purchase or borrow the required textbooks and necessary supplies as soon as possible. The title of the text for your course should be available through the bookstore prior to the beginning of the semester. Plan your schedule to include time to read and study each week. It may be difficult to keep up with the reading, but it is more difficult if you fall behind.

6. Participate: Get to class on time, turn off your phone, and ask questions and share your comments and thoughts regarding the material. It will show you are prepared and engaged in the topic.

DON'T...

1. Be late for class. But if you do arrive late, try to enter the room quietly without distracting the rest of the class.

2. Miss class. If you are going to be absent, contact the professor (prior to missing class if possible).

3. Text or check your phone during class. It's distracting to all.

4. Prepare to leave class before you are dismissed. Putting on your coat or packing your books and computer may be perceived as rude or disrespectful.

5. Talk to a classmate during class.

6. Ask your professor to take responsibility for your absence. Asking "Did I miss anything"? or "Can you send me your lecture notes?" may be perceived as irresponsible. Count on the fact that you did miss material and present to the professor how you plan on making it up (e.g., getting notes from a classmate, attending extra help sessions.)

CHAPTER 2
Learning Styles

HOLLY J. SEIRUP

INTRODUCTION TO LEARNING STYLES/PREFERENCES

Learning is an integral part of life. It begins at birth and is considered, and hoped, to be a lifelong process. The Merriam-Webster Dictionary defines learning as "the knowledge and skills acquired by instruction or study." Learning also involves how someone processes that information, knowledge, and skill. With this in mind, it is important to recognize that everyone does not learn in the same way. In fact, most agree that individuals utilize one of three distinct learning styles or preferences—visual, auditory, or kinesthetic. Keep in mind that there is no right or wrong way to learn, and none of the styles is better than another, nor reflects intelligence. But knowing one's preferred learning style can serve to enhance academic success by increasing effectiveness for learning and study, both in and out of the classroom.

Having a learning preference does not mean that it is the only way someone is able to learn. In fact, it is quite the opposite. College students often find that to be successful in the classroom, they need a variety of learning strategies. This is why it is imperative for students to be aware of what works best for them (which could be quite different from a roommate or friend) and how to go about expanding or strengthening alternative learning strategies and skills. Try the following exercise regarding preference.

In the box below, sign your name…

In the second box sign your name again but this time use the opposite, non-dominant hand.

Consider the differences in the signatures. Most students share that although they can sign there name utilizing either hand, when using their preferred (dominant) hand, they describe the experience as natural, comfortable, easier, taking little extra thought, and faster. When describing using the nondominant hand, they describe the experience as slower, awkward, not as comfortable, needing concentration, attention, and focus. Most agree that with practice they would improve.

The same is true with learning styles. Students have a preferred learning style, which they may find to be comfortable and easy. At the same time they may have found over the years that they also have a need for alternative learning strategies. Perhaps they noticed that their learning style was not aligned with their professors' teaching style or the subject matter being taught. Depending on when they recognized this need, they may have had the opportunity to have practiced and perfected alternative strategies to enhance their effectiveness prior to coming to college. While developing additional strategies may at first be a slower and more complex process requiring more attention and focus, with practice, the ability to utilizing the new strategies improve. This chapter will highlight the characteristics of each of the three learning styles, share strategies to enhance a students' in-classroom and study experiences, as well as review a variety of skills associated with each learning style.

LEFT BRAIN—RIGHT BRAIN

It is hard to discus learning without including information about the brain. The brain has been, and continues to be, widely studied and researched. Discoveries about the brain continue to be made, but we do know that the brain is involved with thinking, learning, and perception. It is broken into two parts, the left brain and the right brain. Once again, people use both sides of the brain but usually have a preference for one side. The dominant side of the brain can have an impact on how one learns.

RIGHT-BRAIN FUNCTIONS
Art awareness
Creativity
Imagination
Intuition
Insight
Holistic thought
Music awareness
3-D forms
Left-hand control

LEFT-BRAIN FUNCTIONS
Analytic thought
Logic
Language
Reasoning
Science and mat
Written
Numbers skills
Righy-hand control

© MedusArt, 2013. Used under license from Shutterstock, Inc.

Left Brain

Those whose left side of the brain is dominant tend to like facts and order. They may be perceived as logical, analytical, and detail oriented, preferring to have information presented and processed sequentially. Characteristics of a left-brain-dominant student might be someone who plans out her study schedule (although she may not follow it), prefers to study alone, and is more likely to have a neat and organized study space.

Right Brain

Those whose right side of the brain is dominant tend to look at things more holistically. They recognize patterns, themes, and spatial relationships. They may be perceived as creative and imaginative and are often comfortable following through on hunches and intuition. Characteristics of a right-brain-dominant student might be someone who prefers to study with others and studies with bursts of energy, which may make him more likely to need to cram at the last minute. His study space is more likely to be cluttered and appear to be unorganized.

It is important to understand that although people may have a dominant side of the brain, both sides are used, so attributes and characteristics from both sides described may be evident in any student. For example, a student may be left-brain dominant, like class material to be presented in a logical and sequential manner, and still have a cluttered workspace.

LEARNING STYLES

There are three different learning styles or preferences: visual, auditory, and kinesthetic. Some times they are alternatively called Reader, Listener, or Doer. There are many assessments available online and in print to assess one's preferred learning style. Overall, to identify learning preference, it is helpful to consider, when given a choice, does one learn best by reading the textbook, listening to a lecture, or by interacting physically with the material?

Visual Learners (Readers)

Visual learners tend to be right-brain dominant and learn more effectively by "seeing" the information presented. This includes reading the textbook and viewing any pictures, graphs, and illustrations related to the material as learning aids. They are likely to take numerous and detailed notes utilizing bullets and highlighters to identify key points, and they can often remember information by visualizing where it appears on a page, in their notes, or in a book. Visual learners tend to have difficulty remaining focused on long lectures and may share that they "zone out" and have difficulty listening, particularly at the end of the lecture. They do a bit better if the professor has a PowerPoint with visuals as part of the presentation. They may also find themselves easily distracted by irritating sounds such as work being done outside of the classroom or classmates talking among themselves during the lecture.

Visual learners tend to be those who may remember people's faces and perhaps what they were wearing when they last met but may not be able to easily recall the person's name. When spelling a word, these students are more likely to write the word down and see if it looks right. They often have a written to-do list and have an organized approach to completing tasks.

Strategies for the Visual Learner   Be aware of the importance of the classroom environment. Visual learners benefit from sitting in the front of the classroom so they can clearly see any diagrams, videos, charts, and graphs. This also allows them to observe the professor's body language and facial expressions, which may be cues to important areas or topics to remember. They need to avoid visual distractions such as anything that obstructs the view (including classmates) and sitting near windows or doors. Visual learners benefit from doing all assigned readings prior to class. While in class, they need to take detailed notes and highlight, underline, and circle key points.

They benefit from copying what the professor writes on the board as a visual cue, participating in discussion to stay involved and attentive in class, and following up by watching any available supplementary videos. Outside of class visual learners do well by finding a quiet place to study, spending some time color-coding notes for clarity, and creating flashcards. Flashcards assist by allowing the learner to see the material, which can serve to reinforce the ability to recall the information in the future.

Auditory Learners (Listeners)

Auditory learners are considered left-brain dominant and learn best by "hearing" the information being presented. They often enjoy listening to a lecture, particularly if the material is presented in a step-by-step, logical sequence. They benefit from class discussion, debates, and study groups where the material is reviewed as it gives these learners an additional opportunity to hear the information. On the other hand, auditory learners may find reading a textbook laborious and slow. They prefer that directions are given to them orally by the instructor as opposed to having to read them, and often these learners may not quickly understand maps, graphs, and diagrams until someone explains the meaning to them.

Auditory learners are often good at remembering people's names once they have been introduced. They often have strong vocabulary skills, may be good at grammar and languages, may have musical talent, and would prefer to give an oral, rather than written, report. When trying to spell a word, these learners are more likely to sound it out. A person who is an auditory learner may summarize and recite facts and readings out loud for clarity and understanding. This helps them to verbalize and hear what they have learned. They may play music to help them concentrate while studying and may hum or talk to themselves. When they make plans for the week, they are more likely to talk them through.

Strategies for the Auditory Learner   If the professor allows, auditory learners benefit from recording lectures and listening to them as part of their study program. (Note that before recording a lecture, students should get permission from the professor.) Attending class is important for all students but particularly for auditory learners because they learn best from hearing the material as opposed to reading about it. When reading the textbook, it is helpful for them to read it aloud or utilize pre-recorded textbooks so the information is heard. In class, students may find it helpful to actively participate in discussions and ask questions for clarification. When studying, it is beneficial for auditory learners to organize study groups to review material, develop rhymes, songs, poems, and mnemonics to assist in memorizing facts, and to recite information out loud, over and over.

Kinesthetic Learners (Doers)

Kinesthetic or tactile learners also tend to be right-brain dominant and learn best by doing. They prefer a hands-on approach where they are actively involved with the material or lesson. They would rather participate in activities and classes that allow them to be active and provide opportunities for discovery, exploration, and experiential learning. These students learn best when they are able to associate abstract material with something more tangible or concrete by applying the information to authentic, real-life situations. They often do well in lab classes, because these allow for the practical application of a lecture.

Kinesthetic learners may have difficulty sitting still and can become restless during long lectures. They may be seen fidgeting, wiggling, or tapping their feet, but this activity helps them stay active and focused. They often doodle in their notes, but their doodles and pictures assist in their learning and recall. The kinesthetic learner likes to solve problems and puzzles, preferably by physically working through them. These students may find it difficult to sit down and read a textbook for extended periods of time. Kinesthetic learners are often successful in careers involving performance, athletics, engineering, art, and acting.

Strategies for the Kinesthetic Learner   The student who is a kinesthetic learner would benefit from identifying classes that provide experiential, hands-on learning whenever possible. They can seek out classes that include demonstrations, fieldwork, trips, museums, and role-play. When in class, they need to find a seat in the room where they can actively participate. They benefit by taking notes "creatively" by using concept maps, the mind-mapping method, drawing pictures, and doodling, all of which assist them in processing and remembering the information.

When studying, it is important for these students to study in shorter blocks of time and take frequent study breaks. Many kinesthetic learners have found it helpful to study in an active and physical manner. Some have found it advantageous to read while on a treadmill, study while taking a walk, squeeze a stress or tennis ball, and/or chew gum while studying or in class. Students may also try studying by using memory games developing flashcards and making learning from the cards into a game (e.g., use the cards to create a memory game such as concentration). Kinesthetic learners may also thrive with a vibrant workspace including music in the background, along with the use of color, posters, and pictures.

HOW MIGHT LEARNING STYLE IMPACT ACADEMIC SUCCESS?

Academic success can be impacted by a student's preferred learning style as well as the professor's teaching style and how those two aspects interact. Many traditional college classes are taught through lecture (which would favor the auditory learner) and readings (which would favor the visual learner.) Today, many professors try to present material and assignments in alternative and multiple methods, recognizing the three learning styles. On the other hand, a student may find that she is in a class that is not being taught in a way she prefers to learn. It is for those circumstances that students are encouraged to identify and understand the strengths and challenges involved in their individual learning preference and whenever possible to practice some of the strategies of the other learning styles.

Understanding one's individual learning style and practicing strategies from the others will maximize a student's learning potential by strengthening his natural abilities and skills, assisting in overcoming limitations, reducing academic frustration and stress, and enhancing motivation and the desire to stay focused on academic success.

CHAPTER 3

Time Management

> *"Time is what we want most, but what we use worst."*
>
> —*William Penn*

TIME

Time for so many is an elusive commodity; something of which we often wish we had more. Yet the fact remains that there are:

- 60 seconds in a minute
- 60 minutes in an hour
- 24 hours in a day
- 168 hours in a week

How one chooses to manage that time is what impacts success. Time management is based upon the recognition and awareness of how one spends time, identifying priorities when time is limited, recognizing and avoiding activities that waste time, and being responsible for the best utilization of time.

WHERE DOES THE TIME GO?

To begin, it is important to identify/analyze how time is spent. For a traditional college student time is most often spent on the following:

Class: Most full-time college students take four to five classes each semester, which would equate to 12–15 hours in class per week.

Studying: It is recommended that for each hour a student spend in class, he spends a minimum of two additional hours outside of class completing the required reading, assignments, reviewing class notes, and working on projects. This equates to 24–30 hours per week. Please note that the 2 hours per hour in class is a minimum and may need to be adjusted based upon the course difficulty, specifics of the assignments, the amount of group work, and preparation needed.

Sleep: Getting enough sleep is important for academic success and overall health. It is recommended that college students get 8 hours of sleep each night. This would equate to 56 hours of sleep per week. Unfortunately, sleep cannot be "banked" for another day. Trying to survive on very little sleep throughout the week and "catching up" on the weekend only makes you tired during the week and impacts your ability to pay attention in class and study. Further excessive sleep on the weekend may make you feel sluggish when you are up and leave you with little time to accomplish your goals.

Work: Many students work while attending college, but whenever possible work hours need to be limited to 15–20 hours. Working over 20 hours per week will impact the amount of time you have to focus on your academics.

Transportation: Student who commute need to budget in the time it takes to get to and from campus as well as how long it takes to park.

Meals: Everyone needs time to eat, and it is recommended that one stops and eats three meals a day. Try not to get caught up with trying to "save time" by getting fast food. Meals may take 14 hours per week, but multitasking is possible by meeting a friend or family member for lunch or dinner.

Exercise: Exercise plays an important role in staying healthy and focused. It needs to be considered as you plan your weekly schedule. Choose something enjoyable and try not to exceed 5–7 hours per week.

Family: Consider time needed for family obligations and responsibilities.

Chores and Personal Hygiene: Schedule in time to complete tasks such as paying bills, shopping for food, cleaning, and personal hygiene such as bathing/showering, shaving, etc.

Flexible Time: It is imperative that some time each week is available for social activities, and spontaneous events. Having some "free" time can help alleviate stress for those working to balance multiple commitments and responsibilities.

Below is an example of analyzing where time goes for a full-time traditional college student who is working and residing on campus.

TIME ANALYSIS EXAMPLE: Where does the time go?

1. In class: (attending full-time taking 5 classes)
   - 5 classes x 3 hours per week   = 15   hours
2. Studying (2 hours for every hour in class)
   - 2 hours of study x 15 hours of class   = 30   hours
3. Sleeping
   - 8 hours per night x 7 nights a week   = 56   hours
4. Working
   - on campus 15 hours per week   = 15   hours
5. Transportation
   - living on campus but drives to visit family and friends   = 3   hours
6. Meals
   - 2 hours per day x 7 days per week   = 14   hours
7. Exercise
   - 1 hour per day x 7days per week   = 7   hours
8. Family obligation/responsibilities
   - Approximately 5 hours per week   = 5   hours
9. Chores/errands/hygiene
   - Approximately 1 hour each day x 7 days per week   = 7   hours

   SUBTOTAL (of hours)   = 152 hours

   ****Hours Remaining for Flexible time 168 – 152*   = 16

10. Flexible time (time with friends, parties, watching TV surfing the web, clubs, intramurals, etc.   = 16   hours

    TOTAL   = 168 hours

Please complete the following exercise.

TIME ANALYSIS WORKSHEET: Where does your time go?

Consider the number of hours you spend on the following each week:

1. In class

   _____# of classes you are taking x _____ # of hours in class per week   =   hours

2. Studying

   _____ 2 hours of study x _____# of hours in class (from #1 above)   =   hours

3. Sleeping

   _____# of hours slept per night x 7 nights per week   =   hours

4. Numbers of hours spent working per week   =   hours

5. Transportation

   _____# of hours spent commuting each day x _____ of days commuting   =   hours

6. Meals

   _____# of hours spent on meals each day x 7 days per week   =   hours

7. Exercise

   _____# of hours spent exercising each day x _____# of days you exercise   =   hours

8. Number of hours spent each week on Family obligation/responsibilities   =   hours

9. Number of hours spent each week on Chores/errands/hygiene   =   hours

   Add up the hours spent on activities to get the SUBTOTAL (of hours)   =   hours

10. Flexible time (time with friends, parties, watching TV surfing the web, clubs, intramurals, etc.) **Subtract your subtotal from the 168 hours available in a week to identify your flexible time**
    168 hours per week - _____your subtotal = flexible hours   =   hours

Often when completing the time analysis exercise, students recognize that they have "too many activities and responsibilities" and not enough time! When adding up the number of hours needed to complete all of their tasks, they exceed the 168 hours in the week. Some will try to negotiate with themselves by cutting back on hours of study and/or hours of sleep or by promising themselves that they will take a shorter shower, only spend 15 minutes a day surfing the web, or stop talking to friends. Yet these decisions may be short sighted and may not be attainable and/or impact the ultimate goal of academic success. When developing a schedule, an honest assessment of how time is spent and setting priorities is imperative to success. It is also important to consider that most activities can be broken down into fixed, daily life, and flexible activities.

Fixed Activities: There are certain activities that are fixed. They are not flexible and must be attended to. For these there are no compromises. These include your class schedule, study time, family responsibilities, meetings, and work that has been pre-scheduled. On the other hand, there is flexibility when deciding how many hours to work and how many activities/meetings to attend. When it comes to flexible or free time, there are decisions to be made that often depend on priorities.

Daily Life Activities: This includes the activities people do to survive and live including such things as sleeping, eating, personal hygiene, chores, paying bills, and shopping. They are necessary and take time but there may be some flexibility with the amount of time spent on these activities. For example personal hygiene - one can take a 5-minute or 30-minute shower.

Flexible Activities: These are activities where there is some discretion. These activities are important and can be very fulfilling. They include spending time with family and friends, volunteer and service activities, and participating in clubs and organizations. It may also include surfing the web, watching TV, and talking on the phone, all of which are activities that may take more time than originally planned, and then may be considered time wasters.

Note Regarding Scheduling Study Time: It is recommended that for every hour spent in class, two additional hours be scheduled outside of class to complete the required reading, assignments, reviewing class notes, and working on class-related projects. This usually equates to between 24 and 30 hours per week. Scheduling these hours effectively can impact the outcome in a course. It is usually best to spread out study time throughout the week as opposed to trying to study 10 hours each day over the weekend. When spreading study time over the week, the student must identify when she is most alert and able to study. For example, a student who identifies himself as a "morning person" would benefit from getting up early and studying before class. Those who prefer and feel energetic in the evening should schedule study time at night. Keep in mind that whatever time is identified as study time, attention should be paid to avoid distractions.

Getting Started: Making a Schedule

Getting organized is the best way to begin on the journey toward effectively managing your time.

1. Identify and choose a method of scheduling and planning activities. This may be in the form of an electronic calendar or a personal (paper) planner. The most important aspect of a planner is making the commitment to use it.
2. Block off your class schedule as well as time to study in the planner.
3. At the beginning of each semester, go through each syllabus, identify all exams, projects, class assignments, and due dates and record them in the planner. This will help to provide an outline or framework for the entire semester and can help to identify times in the semester with particularly high academic demands.
4. Record scheduled work hours, and co-curricular commitments.
5. Add social and family commitments and responsibilities.

Planners are often broken down into months, weeks, and days, which allows for additional organization and scheduling. (Examples and templates can be found at the end of the chapter.)

> **Weekly Schedules:** Many effective time managers also choose to complement their planning by creating weekly and daily schedules. A weekly schedule allows for specific planning based upon the needs, priorities, activities, and tasks of the week. Prior to scheduling, estimates can be made regarding time needed for each task. This may help develop a realistic weekly schedule. The following is an example of a weekly schedule for a traditional college student with a breakdown of time spent on common activities:
>
> In class = 15 hours
>
> Studying = 30 hours
>
> Sleeping = 56 hours
>
> Working = 15
>
> Meals = 14
>
> Transportation = 3
>
> Exercise – 7
>
> Family = 5
>
> Chores/Errands/hygiene = 7
>
> Flexible Time (clubs, friends, parties, etc.) = 16

		Sunday	Monday	Tuesday	Wednesday	Thursday	Friday	Saturday
8	:00 am	Exercise	Exercise	Exercise	Exercise	Exercise	Exercise	Exercise
	:30 am							
9	:00 am	Break fast	Break fast	Break fast	Break fast	Break fast	Break fast	Break fast
	:30 am	Hygiene	Hygiene	Hygiene	Hygiene	Hygiene	Hygiene	Hygiene
10	:00 am	Study	English	Work	English	History	English	Study
	:30 am							
11	:00 am	Study	Spanish	History	Spanish	History	Spanish	Study
	:30 am							
12	:00 pm	Lunch	Lunch	Lunch	Lunch	Lunch	Lunch	Lunch
	:30 pm	Chores/ Errands	Chores/ Errands	Chores/ Errands	Chores/ Errands	Chores/ Errands	Chores/ Errands	Chores/ Errands
01	:00 pm	Study	Work	Work	Work	Work	Study	Study
	:30 pm							
02	:00 pm	Study	Work	Work	Work	Work	Study	Study
	:30 pm							
03	:00 pm	Study	Biology	Philosophy	Biology	Work	Biology Lab	Study
	:30 pm							
04	:00 pm	Trans- port	Club Meeting	Philosophy	Club Meeting	Philosophy	Work	Transport
	:30 pm	Family Time						Work
05	:00 pm	Family Time	Flexible Time	Flexible Time	Flexible Time	Work	Work	Work
	:30 pm		Call Family		Call Family			
06	:00 pm	Dinner	Dinner	Dinner	Dinner	Dinner	Dinner	Dinner
	:30 pm							
07	:00 pm	Family Time	Study	Study	Study	Study	Study	Work
	:30 pm							Transport

		Sunday	Monday	Tuesday	Wednesday	Thursday	Friday	Saturday
8	:00 am	Family Time	Study	Study	Study	Study	Study	Call Family
	:30 am	Transport						Transport
9	:00 am	Study	Study	Study	Study	Study	Flexible Time	Flexible Time
	:30 am							
10	:00 am	Study	Club Meeting	Floor Meeting	Study	Study	Flexible Time	Flexible Time
	:30 am			Call Family				
11	:00 am	Flexible Time	Flexible Time	Flexible Time	Flexible Time	Flexible Time	Flexible Time	Flexible Time
	:30 am							Transport
12	:00 pm	SLEEP	SLEEP	SLEEP	SLEEP	SLEEP	SLEEP	SLEEP
	:30 pm							
01	:00 pm	SLEEP	SLEEP	SLEEP	SLEEP	SLEEP	SLEEP	SLEEP
	:30 pm							
02	:00 pm	SLEEP	SLEEP	SLEEP	SLEEP	SLEEP	SLEEP	SLEEP
	:30 pm							
03	:00 pm	SLEEP	SLEEP	SLEEP	SLEEP	SLEEP	SLEEP	SLEEP
	:30 pm							
04	:00 pm	SLEEP	SLEEP	SLEEP	SLEEP	SLEEP	SLEEP	SLEEP
	:30 pm							
05	:00 pm	SLEEP	SLEEP	SLEEP	SLEEP	SLEEP	SLEEP	SLEEP
	:30 pm							
06	:00 pm	SLEEP	SLEEP	SLEEP	SLEEP	SLEEP	SLEEP	SLEEP
	:30 pm							
07	:00 pm	SLEEP	SLEEP	SLEEP	SLEEP	SLEEP	SLEEP	SLEEP
	:30 pm							

Daily Schedules: These can be considered a to-do list for a particular day. Daily tasks can be identified and then prioritized based upon things that MUST be done that day, important things one would like to get done, and optional things that can get done if time permits.

Setting Priorities: Priorities are set by keeping one's goals in mind. It is also important to identify whether tasks are urgent (A), important (B), or inconsequential (C). Urgent tasks are crucial to your goals; for example, studying for an exam scheduled at the end of the week (crucial to your goal of doing well in the class). An important activity or task is one that is not urgent today but could be in the future. An example of this might be working on a group project that is due at the end of the semester. Finally are the activities or tasks that are neither crucial nor important. These include surfing the web or watching TV for a number of hours.

The following is an example of a daily to-do list.

DAILY TO-DO LIST: Monday

PRIORITY	TASK
A	Study for exam on Friday
B	Arrange a group meeting for end of semester project
A	Submit RA application — deadline Thursday
A	Finish writing assignment due Tuesday
B	Research study abroad opportunities
C	Connect with friends through social media

Identifying What Is Blocking Your Way: Even with the best intentions to effectively manage time, occasionally students find that "something" is blocking their path. Identifying these potential obstacles and developing strategies to overcome them will assist in the development of time management skills. Some of the common barriers are procrastination, feelings of being overwhelmed, distraction, and stress.

Procrastination: According to the Merriam-Webster Dictionary, to procrastinate is "to put off intentionally the doing of something that should be done." Procrastination is a natural and common occurrence occasionally, but it can lead to a cycle where nothing gets done, which may lead to feelings of anxiety, which can impede academic and personal success.

Students procrastinate for many reasons, including:

- **Fear of Failure:** If the task seems daunting and the student lacks confidence that he can complete it successfully, he may decide subconsciously that it's not worth trying to do it at all. To avoid this and get motivated to begin, it is advisable to use positive self-talk and tell yourself "you can complete the task" and "just get started."

- **The Task/Assignment:** Students may find themselves uninterested in the assignment. Perhaps they don't see the relevance to their ultimate academic/career goals. Therefore, completing the task seems like a waste of time. In other situations, they may find the task to be confusing, unpleasant, or difficult. This may be compounded if they are uncomfortable reaching out to the professor for clarification. In these cases, they may keep putting the project "on the back burner."

  In this situation it is important to make a schedule to complete the assignment and stick to it. Timing is important when working on a task that is difficult, it is advisable to begin with the most difficult part of the project first at a time when you are fresh and have the most energy. Schedule breaks, but be cautious not to allow a short break to creep into a time waster. It may also be helpful to identify some type of reward (that doesn't take a lot of time) once a task is complete.

- **Identifying What Is a Priority:** Occasionally, students lose focus on what tasks are most important and timely to complete. They may begin to spend a significant amount of time planning their day, yet this may be a form of procrastinating to avoid getting to work. It is always important to stay focused on your goals and priorities. Some suggest printing these out and keeping them in a place you can see every day.

Feeling Overwhelmed: Students have shared that when they have a lot of tasks to complete, they sometimes begin to feel overwhelmed. They get concerned that they will never be able to complete the projects. This often leads to feelings of anxiety. In this situation, it is advisable to break down the tasks into smaller manageable parts. For example, completing a thesis may seem to be an overwhelming project, but breaking it down into smaller parts and scheduling and completing the smaller parts makes the project more manageable.

Distractions: Distractions can block your ability to get things done. It is important to identify time-wasting distractions. Examples of time wasters are talking on the phone for extended periods of time, responding to text messages while trying to study, engaging with uninvited visitors who stop by when you have scheduled study time. Whenever possible, try to eliminate or reduce time-wasting distractions and stick to your schedule. It may be helpful to find a space on campus conducive to study. Shut off your phone and don't allow yourself to get interrupted by uninvited guests.

Stress: Excessive stress can impact your ability to manage your time effectively. Uncontrolled stress can lead to sickness and multiple health issues. For an in-depth discussion of stress management please see chapter 9.

Helpful Strategies to Enhance Managing Time

Time management is a skill and like many skills it takes practice. There are also many strategies to support using time effectively.

Identify Your Best Study Time: Students are able to study longer and more effectively when they are not tired or distracted. Schedule in study time when you are at your best and have the most energy and focus.

Use Your Waiting Time: Unfortunately, it seems to be a fact of life that there is much time spent each day waiting . . . in line . . . on the phone . . . on a bus/train. Instead of seeing this as a waste of time, with a little preparation it can be used as study time. Use wait time to study from your notes or by creating flash cards. The cards can include vocabulary, key points from a lecture, anything you need to review and/or memorize.

Think of school as your job: If you were not in school you would most likely be working full time approximately 40 hours per week. Consider college as your full-time job and spend the 40–45 hours per week "working" by attending class and studying. Too often, when students first arrive at college, their impression is that they are in class far fewer hours than in high school and have time that they have never had before. (Unfortunately, not appreciating the 2 hours of needed study for every hour in class.) This can lead to falling behind very quickly and may impact academic success.

Try spending a significant part of the day, 8 to 9 hours Monday through Friday, (or less if you can commit time on the weekend) working toward your academic goals.

		Sunday	Monday	Tuesday	Wednesday	Thursday	Friday	Saturday
8	:00 am							
	:30 am							
9	:00 am							
	:30 am							
10	:00 am							
	:30 am							
11	:00 am							
	:30 am							
12	:00 pm							
	:30 pm							
01	:00 pm							
	:30 pm							
02	:00 pm							
	:30 pm							
03	:00 pm							
	:30 pm							
04	:00 pm							
	:30 pm							
05	:00 pm							
	:30 pm							
06	:00 pm							
	:30 pm							
07	:00 pm							
	:30 pm							

DAILY TO DO LIST: Monday

PRIORITY	TASK

CHAPTER 4

Effective Note Taking

> *"If you care about what you do and work hard at it, there isn't anything you can't do if you want to."*
>
> —*Jim Henson,*
> *It's Not Easy Being Green: And Other Things to Consider*

Effective note-taking is one of the fundamental skills impacting students' academic success. Yet it is a skill that is often not taught or practiced in school. Note taking may be considered an art. It allows students to identify patterns and trends and to compare and contrast information that has been presented. It provides students with an overall framework to organize the information acquired in class, discussions, and readings and can serve as a clear and concise study guide.

GETTING STARTED

Note-taking does not commence when a text is opened or the class begins. To be effective, some preparation and planning is needed. Taking notes requires attention and focus. To do this, one must be well rested and work to reduce distractions to be capable of listening and identifying the key points being discussed. Getting enough sleep will assist a student in being able to pay attention to what is being read and/or to what a professor is saying. To reduce distractions it is important to sit in a quiet place surrounded by people who are not talking, fidgeting, or spending time "playing" on their computers or phones. In class it may be helpful to sit closer to the front of the room. This provides a student with the ability to see any visuals being presented, hear the lecture, and actively participate in discussions. Understanding one's individual learning style may also help in choosing the best note-taking method/strategy.

TAKING NOTES

There are a number of ways to take notes, and it is important for students to find the one that best fits their learning style and study requirements. This chapter will be reviewing three effective and common note-taking techniques: (1) traditional outlines, (2) the Cornell method, and (3) mind mapping.

Traditional Outlines

For some, utilizing a traditional outline format can be an effective note-taking method. It is a common method and can be implemented using a formal or informal style. The formal style is considered to be a step-by-step breakdown of material utilizing Roman numerals. The informal style may offer a bit more creativity for students. It uses main subject headings and allows for flexibility in providing supporting information under each heading. This can be done using dashes, arrows, asterisks, or other symbols. Pictures and diagrams can also be included.

Below is an example of the two types of traditional outline note-taking methods using the information in the text regarding note-taking.

Example of a Traditional Outline: Formal

I. Traditional Outlines
  a. Formal
    i. Step by step
    ii. Roman numerals
  b. Informal
    i. Creativity
    ii. Includes main headings
    iii. Utilizes dashes, asterisks, arrows
    iv. Pictures and/or diagrams may be included
II. Cornell Method

Example of a Traditional Outline: Informal

- Creative
- Main headings
- Ex = * - # +
- Charts & diagrams (example below)

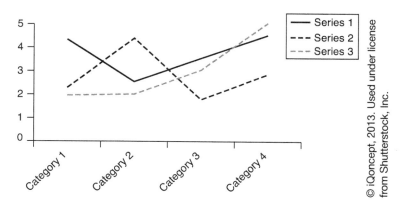

The Cornell Method

The Cornell note-taking method was developed by Walter Pauk of Cornell University. It is an alternative method that includes note-taking, review, and study. To begin, one would divide a page into three sections for notes, cues, and summary.

Basic Structure of the Cornell Method

Cues: Key Points	Notes: Summary

Summary

The notes section is used to record notes from class lectures and discussions. Many find it effective to use the formal or informal outline methods in the notes section. Shortly after class (within 24 to 48 hours), it is important to review notes taken. This will serve to increase one's ability to remember what was discussed in class, it also allows students to check for clarity and understanding as well as fill in any blanks in the notes. While reviewing, the student will complete the Cues section of the page. In the Cues section, the student will write key words, main ideas, possible questions that could be asked on an exam, and any questions he or she has regarding the material. Subsequently, the student will write a summary of the information from the class discussion or lecture in his or her own words. This strengthens the student's understanding of the topic.

Some wonder if spending the time utilizing this method is worthwhile as it moves beyond just taking notes. In fact, the Cornell method can be considered more of a study system. The time spent organizing and reviewing notes after class, as well as periodically prior to an exam, identifying possible exam questions (and identifying how one might answer them) improves likelihood of success. Further, it encourages students to identify questions they may have regarding the topic—early, when they have time to follow up with their professor. Finally, it provides a well-organized study guide that can be used when preparing for a test/exam.

A common study mistake made by students is taking notes and waiting to review them "when needed." Unfortunately, this often occurs right before an exam. When time has gone by, it becomes much more difficult to recall the content of the course lecture, the main points, as well as inhibits the ability to fill in blanks that may be found in notes. This may be compounded if the notes are not legible. Also, if a question regarding the material exists, there may not be time to seek clarification from the professor.

Example using the Cornell method:

Cues: Key Points	Notes: Summary

Notes = Organization
 	
Traditional Outlines
 	
Which method might be better for those who are more creative?
 	
Cornell Method = Notes, Cues, Summary
 	
Which method utilizes a visual, holistic approach?
 	
**Ask Prof: Could you provide further explanation of a holistic approach?
	I. Traditional Outlines
	  a. Formal
	    i. Step by step
	    ii. Roman numerals
	  b. Informal
	    i. Creativity
	    ii. Includes main headings
	    iii. Utilizes dashes, asterisks, arrows
	    iv. Pictures and/or diagrams may be included
	II. Cornell Method
	  a. Notes
	    i. Info from lecture
	    ii. Organize
	  b. Cues
	    i. Main ideas
	    ii. Key words
	    iii. Possible questions
	  c. Summary
	    i. Summary of lecture in your own words
	III. Mind Mapping
	  a. Visual
	  b. Holistic
	  c. See connections, themes

Summary	
Taking effective notes is a way of organizing and understanding course material. It is important to identify a note-taking method (outline, Cornell, mind mapping) that one is comfortable using. Note-taking is a fundamental study skill.	

Mind Mapping

Mind mapping is a note-taking strategy that can assist students to identify and visualize connections and themes. The main idea is placed in the middle and thoughts and subtexts branch out from there. It is considered a holistic way of conceptualizing information and may be favored by right-brain-dominant learners.

Example of Mind Mapping:

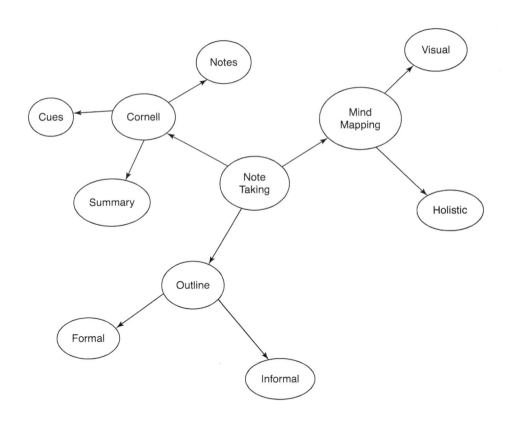

GENERAL TIPS ON NOTE-TAKING

1. Choose a note-taking method. Experiment with the different forms of note taking and choose the one that best fits your learning style and study plan.
2. Prepare. Be prepared to take notes. This includes doing the required reading for class and coming to class well rested.
3. Avoid distractions from your phone, and the people sitting around you. Even your best friends can unintentionally disrupt your thoughts and your ability to pay attention and listen in class.

4. Focus on key words and the main points of a lecture. Professors often give indications of what is important (and potentially on an exam). It may seem intuitive, but listen carefully if you hear phrases such as: "to sum things up . . . , in conclusion . . . , the main point is. . . . "

5. Write clearly and concisely. Try using abbreviations but be sure you remember what they stand for later. Some students try to write down every word a professor is saying and often feel lost and confused as they spend more time focusing on writing every word and not listening to the key points.

6. Review your note as soon as possible after class. Take the time to organize, edit, fill in any blanks, highlight the main concepts, and identify any questions that may need to follow up and discuss with the professor.

7. Review notes often. Don't wait until right before an exam to review your notes. Review after class, before the next class, and periodically throughout the semester to gain the most and support you study efforts.

Course_____ Date_____

TEMPLATE: THE CORNELL METHOD

Cues: Key Points	Notes: Summary

Summary

TEMPLATE—MIND MAP

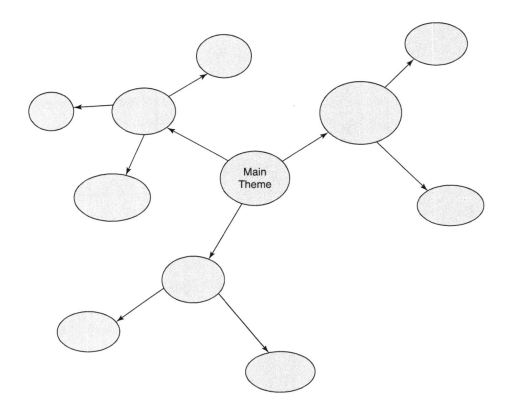

CHAPTER 5

Reading Textbooks

> *"The more that you read, the more things you will know. The more that you learn, the more places you'll go."*
>
> —*Dr. Seuss,*
> *I Can Read With My Eyes Shut!*

Many students find that reading a college textbook takes focus and concentration. Even those who enjoy reading for pleasure often complain of the amount of reading, and the depth of understanding, required to master the material presented in each college-level course. The biggest differences between reading a novel and reading a text is the required level of understanding and the need to retain the information read. Readings in each textbook are assigned to supplement and enhance the material being presented in class. They provide a student with a deeper understanding of the information and ideas that is necessary to synthesize and retain the information to be prepared for class discussion and exams.

Students sometimes find keeping up with assigned readings to be a daunting task because chapters in a textbook are often long, and multiple chapters may be assigned for one topic/class. This chapter will outline the 3R and the SQ3R reading methods, which can be useful for instructing students on how to actively and effectively read a textbook.

THE 3R METHOD: READINESS, READING, AND REVIEW

Readiness: Getting Ready to Read

Although to some this may seem to be implied, preparing to read can often impact one's ability to retain and understand the information. This includes choosing the appropriate environment where reading can occur effectively, the ability to set and reach reading goals, and the importance of previewing the material to be read.

Environment   Choosing a location where one can focus and concentrate on the material is an important way to begin. Some students find reading in their room too distracting either due to noise, interruptions, or the potential to get involved in other projects (see procrastination). Others find they can focus on the reading in their room when sitting at their desk. It is not recommended to try to read lounging on the bed as all too often this leads to a nap as opposed to reading the assigned textbook. Many find leaving their room and reading in the library or a quiet place on campus to be the most effective.

Set Realistic Goals   Decide how many pages and/or chapters will be read during the scheduled study/reading time. It is particularly important to set realistic goals. (It would be unlikely that someone could read 100 pages in half an hour.) When the goal is completed, students find that rewarding themselves with a short break is also helpful.

Preview the Material   Before beginning to read, it is helpful to preview the chapter to get a general idea and overview of what is being introduced. Reading the chapter objectives and the chapter summary can provide students with a general synopsis of what the author is presenting in the chapter.

Reading

Once a student begins to read, he or she needs to read actively. This is often a major change in the approach to reading. Many students have grown up reading passively and attempt to continue to use this approach with a textbook. Unfortunately, they often find this to be ineffective for the learning process. A student who attempts to read passively will often complain that he reads things over and over but the information doesn't seem to "sink in." Active reading includes connecting with and relating to the material by identifying initial questions about the information and looking for evidence to answer the questions raised. It includes identifying key words and phrases, highlighting important facts and concepts, and discovering new vocabulary. Students who are active readers are more likely to retain and process the information read. Subsequently, they are able to draw on that information when needed for class discussion or on an exam.

Identifying Questions: Many students use the chapter headings to begin to identify questions relating to the material. For example the first major heading in this chapter is "Readiness: Getting Ready to Read." Possible questions for this section of the reading would be, "Why is it important to get ready to read?" or "How can one get ready to read?" When the student completes the section of the chapter, he or she attempts to answer questions from the material presented. This provides an opportunity to be actively engaged in the reading and learning process.

Exercise: Changing a Heading into a Question: Please change the headings below into possible questions.

1. The dangers of smoking cigarettes

   _____

2. Martin Luther King, Jr.

   _____

Key Words or Phrases   Key words or phrases in the chapter that are **bolded**, highlighted, and/ or in *italic* are presented in that manner because they are important. Students will benefit from making sure that they understand the words and phrases that have been emphasized.

Vocabulary   When students come across an unfamiliar word, it is recommended that they write it down and look up the definition for increased understanding. To further increase and enhance vocabulary, it is recommended that the word and definition be put on an index card and reviewed periodically. Students may also find that attempting to use the word in conversation/ discussion assists in committing the word to memory.

Highlighting   Many students find highlighting important aspects of a chapter to be an effective method to identify key points and assist in learning the material. Unfortunately, highlighting can be overdone, and some find that after completing the reading the majority of the chapter is highlighted, thus decreasing the effectiveness and purpose. Students may also find it helpful and may want to consider using a pen or pencil to add notes directly in the margins of the text. Key points can be identified with asterisks or exclamation points. If there is something unclear, a question mark can be placed in the margin to identify a topic for further review.

Review the Reading

After completing the chapter, the next step is to review. This allows the student to paraphrase what was read, make connections and integrate with the notes from class, and ultimately retain the information. Take time to answer any questions, exercises, or problems that may be included at the end of the chapter.

SQ3R METHOD

A very popular and often used reading method is SQ3R: Survey, Question, Read, Recite, and Review.

Survey

The survey section of the SQ3R method offers students the opportunity to identify the purpose and gain an overview of the chapter being read. The survey process should take between

5 and 15 minutes. The student would begin by reading the chapter introduction and summary. This is the first step in providing connections between the main ideas being presented. Next, the student would review the chapter headings, which can give a hint about the structure of the chapter, followed by a review of any visuals such as pictures, charts, diagrams, and graphs, which are often utilized to illustrate important points and facts. Reviewing any questions provided at the end of a chapter can identify areas that need particular focus when reading the text. Many find that getting an understanding of the chapter as a whole assists the reader in understanding how the various parts of the chapter fit together.

Question

Similar to the previous method, the SQ3R method recommends that students develop questions out of the major heading in the topic. Questions should be clear and concise, using the key words *who*, *what*, *when*, *why*, and *how*. After reading each section, the student answers the questions. For example, the heading of this section of the chapter is "SQ3R Method." Possible questions might be "How can I use the SQ3R method?" or "What is the SQ3R method?" When students complete reading the information on the SQ3R method, they should be able to answer these questions.

Read

Students must read one section at a time. After completing a section, they try to answer their initial questions in their own words. If they have difficulty answering the question, it is important to reread that section. If the section is still unclear, it may be an area to review with the professor during office hours.

Recite

It often helps to "hear" important facts. Summarizing a section of the reading out loud may increase retention of the material. If, after reading a section, a student cannot summarize the material, it is a clear indication that comprehension of the topic has not been mastered and that the section should be reread for clarity.

Review

It is best to review the reading (either the notes you have taken or the highlighted or marked sections in the chapter) within 24 hours and periodically prior to an exam. This will enhance retention and recall of the information and promote academic success.

READING STRATEGIES/TIPS

1. Schedule time to complete reading assignments. Be realistic and identify shorter blocks of time when your energy level is high. It may be more effective to schedule two blocks of 2 hours each than one 4-hour block to read.

2. Concentrate. It is easier to read when you are well rested. It is also important to avoid distractions. If you find yourself dozing off or your mind drifting, try reading out loud. If this persists, it may be time for a short break. Get up, stretch, and/or take a short walk then get back on task.

3. Location . . . location . . . location. Find a quiet, well-lit spot with few distractions where you are comfortable reading. (Not too hot and not too cold.)

4. Highlight important concepts but not every word. Underlining or highlighting can give some a false sense of security. Keep in mind that highlighting does not equate to learning or understanding.

5. Be an active reader. Create questions from the headings and answer the questions based upon what you have read. Summarize and synthesize the material—out loud whenever possible.

6. Connect what you are reading with the notes from class. This allows for a concise and thorough study guide.

7. Consider joining or organizing a study group to discuss the assigned reading. This can enhance clarity and understanding.

8. If you have any remaining or additional questions about the material, speak to your professor.

© wavebreakmedia, 2013. Used under license from Shutterstock, Inc.

CHAPTER 6

Writing Skills

> *"To me, the greatest pleasure of writing is not what it's about, but the inner music that words make."*
>
> —*Truman Capote*

DEVELOPING THE ART OF WRITING

Developing strong writing skills is an important factor impacting a students' overall academic success. Writing provides the opportunity to organize one's thoughts regarding relationships and ideas and share them with others. It is a skill that may or may not have been developed and strengthened during K–12 education, yet it is important in the majority of classes taken on the collegiate level. Some students find that in high school, writing is focused in English and perhaps history classes, where in college writing skills are expected in classes across the curriculum.

Students often enter college with a preconceived idea about what kind of writer they are usually based upon past experiences. Some are quite confident that they have excellent writing skills and are unconcerned when entering college. Some are quite skilled in writing, having spent a lot of time practicing and preparing for future work. Others may have received good feedback and grades when in high school and have been able to follow a rubric such as the five-paragraph essay. Unfortunately, they may not have developed the necessary skills of analysis, research, and style to be successful in a college course. They might be quite surprised and have their confidence shaken to find that they are receiving very different feedback and grades once in college.

On the other hand, some students are convinced that they are not good writers and may find it difficult and perhaps overwhelming when they realize the amount of writing required in many college-level

courses. This chapter will review writing skills and provide additional resources to improve or enhance students' current writing skills.

THE WRITING PROCESS

Writing is a process. It takes time and preparation. A common mistake students make is when they believe that they can just sit down right before an assignment is due and produce a quality paper. Unfortunately, this rarely works. Following the steps outlined in the text will enhance one's ability to write. This includes taking time to prepare to write; organizing your thoughts, ideas, and material; writing; reviewing; editing; and proofreading.

Step 1: Prepare

The first step is preparing to write. To do so, one must ensure there is an understanding of the assignment or prompt. A student may be asked to analyze, compare and contrast, discuss, or summarize a topic. Depending on what is being asked may change the focus and writing of the essay.

Review of possible prompts for writing assignments

Analyze: Break down various parts of the material and relate it back to the whole. For example, analyzing two short stories may involve looking at the various parts of the stories (plot, character development, setting, and themes) and connecting them back to the overall theme of the story or class topic.

Compare and Contrast: Focus on the similarities and differences. For example, if asked to compare and contrast WWI and WWII, one would highlight what aspects of the wars were the same and what were different.

Discuss: Give an overview of the topic and provide examples. If the prompt was to "discuss life in the United States during WWII" a student would describe life during that time using examples (e.g., women working in factories to support the war effort, food rations)

Summarize: Provide an overview of the main ideas and how they fit together.

Some students find that the most difficult essays are those with no prompt—where the topic is open. In these circumstances it is recommended that a student brainstorm possible topics, focusing in on what she has found interesting about the class subject matter, what has left her wondering, or if she has any unanswered questions. Something that has piqued her curiosity. For example, a student is enrolled in a psychology class with an assignment to write an essay/paper on a related topic of his choice. The student would review the topics presented in class (e.g., Freud's dream analysis) and consider topics where he still has questions (e.g., Is dream analysis used today? If so, how?).

A common mistake made when identifying an essay/paper topic is making the idea too broad. When the topic is too wide ranging, identifying the themes to support the topic will be unwieldy and often impossible to complete effectively in one essay or paper. For example, if the assignment for an economics class was to write an essay that compares and contrasts two historical aspect of the U.S. economy, a student would begin by brainstorming possible topics by reviewing subjects discussed in class, assigned readings, and research current literature that has been written on the topic (U.S. economy). Perhaps there are a number of areas of interest, but the writer needs to begin to focus on one area such as the stock market. Yet, the stock market is still too broad a topic. The decision could be made to focus in on times when the market crashed. This would allow the student to discuss the circumstances in each crash and compare and contrast the two. The process of sifting through possible topics and whittling it down to a more specific and manageable content area is important in the essay development and also helps to identify the thesis statement.

Assignment: Write an essay that compares and contrasts two historical aspect of the U.S. economy.

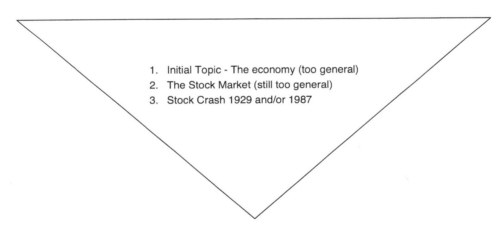

1. Initial Topic - The economy (too general)
2. The Stock Market (still too general)
3. Stock Crash 1929 and/or 1987

Thesis: The 1929 stock market crash had a larger impact on the U.S. economy than the crash in 1987.

Step 2: Organize

Organization is an important but often overlooked step in the writing process. It is uncommon for anyone to sit down at the computer, or with a blank pad of paper, and have the ability to complete the writing assignment effectively. Taking time to organize one's thoughts and ideas into a general outline can serve as a foundation to the completion of the essay/paper. Spending time developing an outline can actually save time as research is being gathered and/or information is being collected to support the main points.

Outline Utilizing the Stock Market Example

I. Introduction
   a. Include overview of the main points that will be presented
   b. Thesis statement

II. Stock Market Crash of 1929
    a. Factors leading up to the 1929 crash
    b. Impact of the crash
    c. Recovery

III. Stock Market Crash of 1987
    a. Factors leading up to the 1987 crash
    b. Impact of the crash
    c. Recovery

IV. Comparison and Contrast
    a. What were the similarities of the two crashes?
    b. What were the main differences?

V. Conclusion
    a. Restate the main points
    b. Provide a final and concise statement to support or deny the thesis statement

It is also helpful to plan a schedule to complete the writing assignment. This includes all the steps of the writing process. It will take time to thoroughly research and gather enough information on each of the areas in the outline. Further, it is necessary to identify time to review and edit work once it is written.

Step 3: Write

There are three main parts of an essay, whether you are writing in class, on an exam, or for a paper. They are the introduction, the body, and the conclusion.

Introduction   The introduction explains to the reader what the paper is about, its overall content. In the introduction the writer hopes to convince readers why the topic is important and get them interested so that they want to continue reading. It includes a clear and concise thesis statement or research question(s).

Body   In the body of the paper or essay, the various themes related to the overall topic are introduced and discussed as they relate to the thesis statement or research question. Evidence is provided to support the themes and assertions made. Supporting evidence can be obtained from credible sources such as reviewing current literature, course readings, and lecture notes. The body of the paper is also the place to provide relevant details, examples, and statistics to support the main themes.

There is no set number of paragraphs, but the writer tries to focus each paragraph on one theme in a concise yet thorough manner. Smooth transitions between topics and paragraphs are integral to the flow of the paper/essay.

Conclusion   The conclusion is an opportunity to summarize and restate the main themes of the paper in a clear and logical format, which is related to the original thesis statement or research question. Did the writer make the argument to support or deny his or her thesis statement? Did he or she answer the research question? For example, in the conclusion section of the paper on the stock market, the thesis statement was "The 1929 stock market crash had a larger impact on the U.S. economy than the crash in 1987." After reading the paper, the reader should be convinced that this is either true (argument was made to support the thesis statement: The 1929 stock market crash had a larger impact on the U.S. economy than the crash in 1987) or false (argument was made to deny the thesis statement: The 1929 stock market did not have a larger impact on the U.S. economy than the crash of 1987). The conclusion may also include a "call to action", implications, and/or areas for future research.

The Writing Process: Identifying Ideas, Developing a Thesis Statement, Organizing the Research, Conclusion

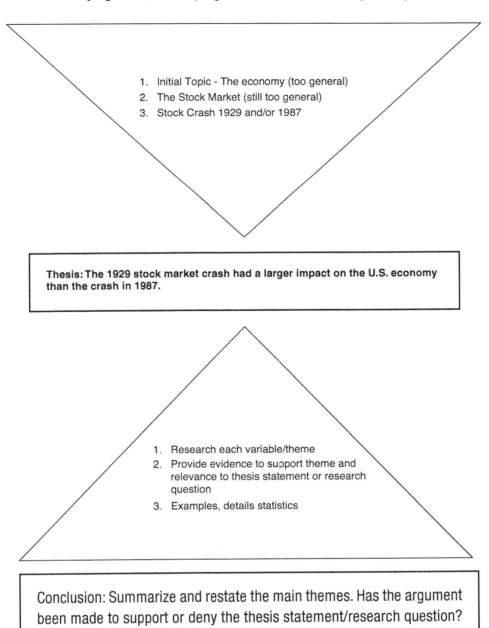

REVIEW

Once the first draft is complete, the next step is to review and edit. It is strongly recommended at this point that the paper is printed and proofread. It is not wise to rely entirely on the word processing programs when it comes to grammar and spell check. There are times when a word is spelled correctly but may not be the right word. For example, if an argument was being weather the 1929 stock market crash impacted the U.S. economy, the word *weather* is spelled correctly, but the writer meant to use *whether*. Confirm that all abbreviations used in drafting the paper or taking notes are removed and replaced with the full word (e.g., change U R to you are). It may be helpful to read the paper out loud or, if time permits, have a peer review the paper for flow. Confirm that citations and the bibliography are in the correct format as outlined by the professor. Commonly used formats are MLA (Modern Language Association) and APA (American Psychological Association). If you are unaware of how to use the style required by your professor, seek assistance from the writing center or an academic advisor.

NOTE ABOUT PLAGIARISM

When completing a writing assignment, it is sometimes tempting to copy or "cut and paste" from someone else's paper. Using someone else's work as you own, without properly citing the work, is plagiarism and a clear violation of campus policy on academic integrity. With the amount of information available on the Internet, copying sentences, paragraphs, and even entire papers has grown exponentially as have the ways of identifying the plagiarism through software such as turnitin.com. Schools at all levels value academic integrity and hold each member of the community (students and faculty) to a high standard. It is the students' responsibility to know and understand the policy. If there are any questions, it is imperative to seek clarification from one of the many academic support services available on campus.

SUPPORT SERVICES

Many students find that they need some assistance with a part of the writing process. Students are encouraged to seek assistance through the writing center, tutorial services, and the center for Academic Advisement or by utilizing online resources such as the Purdue online writing lab at http://owl.english.purdue.edu/owl.

CHAPTER 7

Taking Tests

> "You must expect great things of yourself before you can do them."
>
> —*Michael Jordan*

TESTS

The administration of some type of test or exam as a means of assessing student learning has become a typical part of a college-level course. Tests may come in a variety of formats, yet the goal is to assess the level of mastery and understanding of the material that has been presented. People approach testing in different ways. Some view it as a challenge to be won; others find it to provoke anxiety and stress.

One of the greatest differences students may notice between high school and college is the number of tests administered during a quarter or semester. In high school, tests are often given at the end of each major topical unit that is presented. The information, therefore, is often fresh in a students' mind; most have likely attended the majority of the classes and completed related homework and in-class assignments. In a college course, testing is often done quite differently. Tests and exams might be limited, at times, having only two—a mid-term and a final each weighing significantly toward the final grade. This places additional pressure on a student to do well. For a first-year student who sees that the first exam is seven weeks into the semester, keeping up with readings and assignments might be put off because it seems like there is lots of time before the exam. Nontraditional students may have difficulty keeping up due to the multiple demands they have (e.g., family obligations, working full-time) above and beyond class requirement. Yet one of the first things to consider in test preparation is that it begins right away—the first day of class. It includes:

- Attending class regularly
- Keeping up with readings, assignments, and homework
- Reviewing notes and assigned reading early, often, and regularly before an exam

It also means taking advantage of university resources early such as requesting a tutor, attending available review sessions and supplemental instruction, and visiting professors during office hours when questions arise.

Before the Test

Before any test or exam it is necessary to prepare physically, emotionally, and cognitively.

Physically   In order to stay focused and able to study for an exam, it is necessary to get enough sleep, maintain an exercise routine, and eat well. Not getting enough sleep will impact concentration throughout your study schedule and during an exam. Avoid the temptation to replace your study plan by pulling an "all-nighter" full of cramming. As expected, cramming for an exam is an ineffective study plan and should only be utilized as a last resort. Staying up all night only leaves one drowsy and having difficulty concentrating during the exam. It is recommended that a student get between 6 and 8 hours of sleep prior to an exam. Further, maintaining a moderate exercise routine throughout the semester is important to academic success. Some students discover that when they let their exercise program lapse due to time constraints, they find that they begin to feel sluggish and inattentive when studying. On the other hand, spending too much time exercising (2 to 4 hours a day) may also lead to exhaustion and may be used as a form of procrastination.

Maintaining healthy eating habits is also important when preparing and taking an exam. Living on junk food, sugar, and caffeine may temporarily cause feelings of alertness and comfort, but ultimately this habit can trigger feelings of lethargy and lack of focus in a student. It is recommended that students eat a well-balanced meal before an exam. This will increase the probability that the student is not distracted during the exam with hunger pains, headaches, and/or feeling faint.

Emotionally   It is critical that students take care of themselves emotionally. This can directly impact test preparation and results. A moderate amount of time to relax should be scheduled into the study plan. This might mean taking a short break each day to do something one really enjoys and finds relaxing. It is important for students to recognize that this means a "moderate amount of time" to relax. They must be cognizant of the temptation of extending a break and suddenly finding themselves wasting time, which could lead to procrastination, making it much more difficult to get back on their study schedule.

Maintaining a positive attitude about the test is also important. This can be done by reframing negative thoughts into ones that are more positive by using positive self-talk. For example, when thinking "I'm going to fail this exam," reframe the statement and say "I will do well on this exam."

Exercise: Reframing—Using Positive Self-Talk

Please reframe each of the statements into one that is more positive

1. Initial Statement: I'll never finish what I need to study for the exam.

   Positive Reframe: _____

2. Initial Statement: I know I'm not prepared enough for the test.

   Positive Reframe: _____

Cognitively   As the date of the scheduled exam gets closer, it is important to find out from the professor the details regarding the test, including:

- What topics will be on the exam?
- Will the exam be cumulative?
- What type of questions should be expected (e.g., multiple choice, fill in, essay)?
- Is the exam open or closed book?
- Will there be a review session(s)?

Knowing the answers to these questions can alleviate some anxiety and assist in test preparation. It is also essential to identify and utilize all available resources, including:

- Attending formal review sessions organized by the professor and informal ones with classmates
- Joining a study group
- Completing practice tests if available and sanctioned by the professor
- Reviewing questions or problems in the text
- Developing a study plan/schedule and sticking with it

Creating a valuable study plan includes breaking down the information that will be on the exam into manageable sections and scheduling times to review each section in smaller blocks of time. Many find it difficult to study 6 straight hours but identifying two blocks of 3 hours or three blocks of 2 hours may seem more manageable. Study time needs to be included in one's weekly and/or monthly calendar. Planning ahead, scheduling appropriate blocks of time, and sticking to the schedule can avoid cramming, and the last-minute study frenzy.

Identifying an appropriate study space with few distractions can enhance one's ability to review and retain the information needed for the exam. Some other useful tips include utilizing mnemonics, visualization, and flash cards. *Mnemonics* is the use of rhymes, jingle, acronyms, and songs to help one remember facts and content. For example, "Columbus sailed the ocean blue in 1492" is a well-known rhyme that assists many in remembering when Columbus sailed. Some find utilizing or creating acronyms a useful memory aid. For example, memorizing SQ3R may help to jog one's memory to remember that it stands for Survey, Question, Read, Recite, and Review. Students often find that they are more able to remember facts and figures if they create a jingle, rhyme, or acronym regarding the material.

Exercise: Mnemonics

Try creating a rhyme out of the following information.

Robert Frost wrote many poems. Create a rhyme that might help you remember the names of these two poems.

"A Prayer in Spring"

"The Road Not Taken"

On the day of the test it is recommended to get a good night's sleep (6 to 8 hours). If the exam is early in the morning, consider setting more than one alarm. Waking up late means rushing to an exam, which for most people increases any level of anxiety. Plan to get to the classroom at least 5 minutes early to get organized and relax. Allow for driving and parking delays. Bring the supplies needed for the exam (e.g., a calculator, multiple pens, and/or pencils) Get ready . . . take a deep breathe and begin.

During the Test

When the exam is first distributed to the class, it is recommend that students begin by surveying the entire exam, identifying what types of questions and how the points are distributed throughout the test. If there is a particular concept that a student feels he might have difficulty remembering, he may want to consider writing it down somewhere on the exam in pencil to refer to at a later point and where it can be erased upon completion. The next step is to make sure to put one's name on the test and then read and follow the directions carefully. Begin by answering what might be considered the "easy" questions first (this often serves to build confidence), followed by those with the highest point value. This increases the probability of receiving the most possible points if the exam is not completed. If a student gets stuck on a question, it is best to move on and return to the question if time permits after completing the remaining questions. Once the exam is completed, take time to review. There is no rush to leave the classroom early. In variably, there is one person in a class who seems to complete the exam in "record time." For some students remaining, this can increase their anxiety and stress. In fact, there does not seem to be a correlation between finishing early and a high grade on the exam. It is more important to use the time allotted to complete and review the exam.

Types of Tests and Test Questions

There are many different types of tests and test questions. The most common forms are the in-class, open book, and take-home exams. For tests administered in class, there are often a mix of subjective (multiple choice, true-false, fill-in, and matching) and/or objective (short answer and essay) type questions. For take-home exams the most common are the subjective questions/style.

Objective   Objective-type tests and questions most commonly include true-false, multiple choice, fill-in-the-blank questions, and matching. These questions most often are testing the students' ability to learn facts and concepts from the course material. There is usually one correct answer to the question. If the student does not identify the correct answer, it is marked wrong. Once an answer is chosen, it is usually best not to change it unless one realizes that the question was misread initially and the student is now confident the answer is wrong.

Subjective   Subjective test questions usually include short answer and essay questions. In these questions the person correcting the test may use some subjectivity, his or her opinion, as to whether the answer is correct. The student might be asked to write his or her opinion and support it with evidence. The professor would make a judgment as to how well students were able to achieve that goal. It may be possible to receive partial credit for a well-written response.

Open Book and Take Home Tests   Many students initially feel relieved when they find that a class requires an open book or take-home exam. Some believe that these types of exams take some pressure off the need to study, yet that thought is false. These exams are often more challenging because the professor has higher expectations of the work submitted by students. The study plan and preparation should be the same.

Tips for Answering Different Types of Questions

True-False   Read the question carefully and keep in mind that to be marked as true, every part of the statement must be true. Be aware of qualifier words such as "always," "never," and "every" because these statements are usually false. For example, the statement: "It always snows in the winter in the northeast portion of the United States" is false. It usually snows in the winter, but

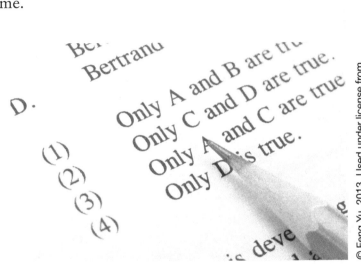

there have been winters with no snow. On the other hand, statements with words such as "occasionally," "usually," and "some" are usually true. Going back to the snow statement: "It usually snows in the winter in the northeast portion of the United States" is true. If one is completely unsure of the answer and leaving it blank will count as incorrect, take a guess—there is a 50-50 chance of getting it correct.

Multiple Choice   Start by reading the question carefully and formulating an answer before looking at the possible answers provided. Once an answer is formulated, look at the possible answers from which to choose. If the answer you formulated is one of the choices listed, it would be the best choice. If it is not, begin to eliminate choices that are obviously incorrect or not relevant. Of the remaining possible answers choose the best fit.

Multiple Choice Example:

1. It usually snows in the winter in what part of the United States?

   A. Patagonia

   B. Northeast

   C. South

   D. All of the above

To approach this question, one would read the question and formulate an answer before looking at the four choices provided. One might decided that it usually snows in the winter in the northeast, northwest, or northern parts of the United States. The next step is to find if one of the answers formulated is in the list of choices. In this example it is, and the student would choose B. Northeast.

At the same time, if the student was unsure of an answer, he or she could eliminate answers that were obviously wrong or irrelevant. In this example, A. Patagonia could be eliminated because it in South America, not in the United States. Since A is not correct, D, all of the above, cannot be correct. This leaves two choices B. Northeast, and C. South. From this point there is a 50-50 chance of choosing the correct answer.

Be aware of questions that use the words "except" and "not." For example, "All of the following are true EXCEPT . . . ." or "Which of the following is NOT related to . . . ." These can be confusing and some students regard them as trick questions. They are not tricky if you are aware of them and identify them while reading the question.

Fill-in   With fill-in questions it is best to look for cues in the statement or question. Cues might include grammar, tense, the number of or length of the blank space(s). Leaving a fill-in blank usually counts as an incorrect answer, therefore it is recommended to take a chance and perhaps try to explain your answer in the margin of the exam. Fill-ins are often based on vocabulary, facts, and concepts. If one knows fill-in questions will be on an exam, utilizing flash cards as a study aid may be very helpful.

Fill-in Example

It usually snows in the winter in the Northeast portion of the _____   _____.

Answer: Including two spaces in the fill-in usually implies that answer is two words. This is a cue, which can be used to help identify the answer of "United" and "States."

Matching   Matching usually occurs between two columns of related material. For example, vocabulary words might be on one side and definitions on the other. It is recommended to match the ones that one is confident about first and look for clues to either eliminate or match the remaining material.

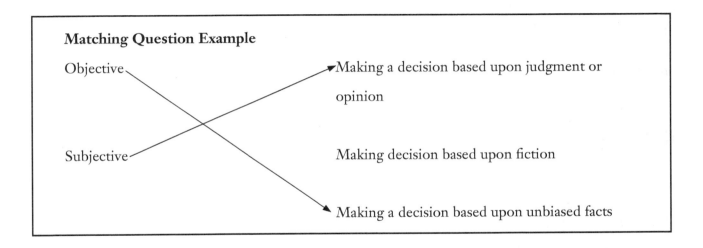

Matching Question Example

Objective

Subjective

Making a decision based upon judgment or opinion

Making decision based upon fiction

Making a decision based upon unbiased facts

Subjective (Short Answer)   Short answers on an exam provide an opportunity for a student to demonstrate to the professor that he or she has a grasp of the material and can communicate it in a clear and concise fashion. If a student is unaware of the answer, it is best to make an attempt because short answers usually carry more points and usually the possibility for partial credit.

Subjective (Essay)   Similar to the short answer, the essay question gives a student the opportunity to demonstrate mastery of the course material. It is analogous to a short version of writing a paper and can be approached in a similar way. The same process of organizing one's thoughts and material, developing a quick outline focusing on the important points to be included, and a well-formulated conclusion will assist in presenting a well-written, thorough essay. This may not be the time to write down everything you know about a broad topic. Try to stay focused on answering the question that is asked and use related facts, examples, and supporting evidence. At times students can get very involved when answering an essay question. It is important to budget one's time to be able to complete the exam on time. Do all possible to write clearly, concisely, and legibly. This will make it easier for the professor to read, understand, and evaluate what the student has written.

NOTE ABOUT TEST ANXIETY

A certain amount of anxiety or stress is natural when facing life's challenges. It can serve to motivate a person to work hard and succeed. On the other hand, too much stress can hinder one's ability to be effective and to achieve one's goals. In testing situations, a modest amount of stress/anxiety might motivate a student to develop and stick to her study plan; too much may inhibit a student's ability to do well on the exam. The symptoms of anxiety can range from sweaty palms and a feeling of "butterflies" in the stomach to feelings of heart palpitations, panic, and blanking out on a test.

To reduce test anxiety, it is important to do all possible to be prepared physically, emotionally, and cognitively, including developing and sticking to a study plan. Use all study strategies and resources available. Try to stay calm using deep breathing before and during the exam. Dispute negative thoughts by replacing them with positive ones such as "I can do this." If the anxiety begins to impact the ability to do well on an exam or encroaches into other parts of one's life, it is imperative to seek professional help at the student counseling center.

NOTE ABOUT CHEATING

No matter how tempting it might be to glance at someone else's exam, it is never a good alternative. When entering a college or university, students commit to following certain academic standards. Many colleges and universities have students sign an honor code, pledge, or statement where they agree to abide by the academic integrity policy of the school. Schools take this very seriously and violations of the policy can lead to sanctions including failing a specific assignment, failing the entire course, up to suspension and expulsion from the school. Not knowing the policy or the definition of what is academic dishonesty is not an excuse to cheat or plagiarize. Policies are often included on course syllabi and information is available on campus websites. Students need to take some time to review and understand the policy, and if they have any questions, speak to their academic advisor of faculty member.

AFTER THE TEST

After completing an exam or submitting an assignment, students are encouraged to reward themselves for a job well done with a healthy treat (e.g., seeing a movie, spending time with friends). When the test is returned by the instructor, a thorough review of the test is recommended. This is an important step because it helps students identify common mistakes made on the exam. Was there a specific type of question consistently gotten wrong? Was there an area that was not studied completely? Ultimately, the purpose of reviewing the test is to assess whether the study plan/strategy worked for the student. If it did, continue to use it, if it did not, make the necessary modifications/changes prior to the next exam.

If a student believes that the exam did not adequately demonstrate his knowledge of the subject matter, or if he did not do as well as he would have liked, it might be helpful to speak to the professor to inquire what he can do to perform better on the next exam and in the class overall. The exam should be used as a learning tool for future tests in a particular class and for future classes.

CHAPTER 8

Developing and Maintaining Healthy Relationships Communication Skills

> *"People fail to get along because they fear each other; they fear each other because they don't know each other; they don't know each other because they have not communicated with each other."*
>
> —*Martin Luther King, Jr.*

Developing and maintaining healthy relationships don't just happen, the process often takes time and energy, along with a genuine commitment to build associations. It includes employing active and assertive communication skills, responding promptly and effectively when conflicts arise, developing trust and exhibiting respect, as well as valuing and seeking out relationships with those who are different from oneself. The collegiate experience offers many opportunities for students to formulate new and lasting relationships. Taking advantage of the opportunities provided and learning the skills necessary to develop and strengthen those relationships is the focus of this chapter.

THE FOUNDATION OF RELATIONSHIPS–COMMUNICATION SKILLS

Communication skills are the foundation for building and maintaining relationships. It is often said that communication is the key to success academically, professionally, and personally. Since it is a learned skill, with practice one can improve in this area. This is important as an extensive amount of time each day is spent communicating. But what is communication? Communication can be defined as the exchange of information, ideas, and feelings. The concept of exchange illustrates giving and receiving. For communication to be effective, it has to be a two-way process. It includes speaking, listening, and understanding by all involved in the interaction. Problems and conflict can arise due to miscommunication when the message is not shared or heard clearly. This can be caused by failing to speak distinctly, failing to listen, and/or a lack of understanding of the message or feeling being conveyed.

For many college students, miscommunication has been compounded by electronic communication such as social media and text messaging. Although electronic communication provides the text of the message, it lacks the nuance of meaning, voice tone, and perhaps humor.

Unfortunately, without such context, messages can be misunderstood, leading to conflict and/or hurt feelings. Subsequently, such conflict can impede a student's ability to focus on academics and may impact his or her overall campus experience.

GENERAL COMMUNICATION STRATEGIES

Active Listening

The Greek philosopher Epictetus' famous quote (which has been repeated and passed down by parents and teachers for centuries) states, "We have two ears and one mouth so that we can listen twice as much as we speak." Yet all too often, people try so hard to get their point across that they talk more than they listen. When another is speaking, they spend the time thinking of their response rather than listening to what is being said. Much of the message is lost in these types of interactions. Listening involves staying focused on what the other person is saying without interrupting and without distractions (including contemplating a response).

© Sukhonosova Anastasia, 2013. Used under license from Shutterstock, Inc.

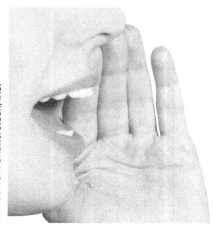 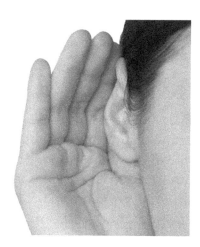

Nonverbal Communication

Probably the most important factor in effective communication is the ability to listen—really listen attentively and actively. This involves listening to the total message being conveyed including the words (verbal message) as well as the way it is being shared through body language (nonverbal message) through voice tone, facial expression, and gestures. Nonverbal language can add context, which can help in understanding the message. Inconsistencies in the verbal and nonverbal messages should be explored. For example, if a friend is sharing that she failed an exam and looks close to tears, the message probably is that she is upset about failing the exam. If the same person failed the exam but is smiling and laughing, it might be worthwhile to discuss the inconsistency between the verbal and nonverbal message in more detail. If the message were sent via electronic methods such as a text, "I failed my exam," it would be difficult to fully understand the total message, including how the person is feeling about or responding to the situation.

Listeners also need to be aware of their nonverbal communication. If a listener is hearing something very sad yet maintains a smiling face, it could be perceived that he is not fully listening or hasn't heard the message. Therefore, listeners are encouraged to pay attention to their own body language as well as observing that of others. It is necessary to be aware of possible cultural differences in the meaning of body language. For example, in some cultures lowering one's eyes or avoiding eye contact might be perceived as avoiding a situation or exhibiting feelings of being ashamed or embarrassed. Yet in other cultures the same action/behavior is a sign of respect. Cultural differences need to be recognized and respected.

Clarification and Paraphrase

While listening, there may be times when the message is not understood. In these situations it is very appropriate to ask for clarification to insure understanding. Using statements such as: "Can you elaborate on . . .?" "Tell me more about . . ." encourages further discussion, which can assist in clarifying the situation. Paraphrasing is another useful skill. It involves listening to someone's message and repeating it back in your own words. Paraphrasing what someone has said is also a good way to confirm that you truly understand the message being conveyed. For example, "Let me make sure I understand what you said . . . [paraphrase—repeat the message being conveyed in own words]."

A Good Listener—Finding Common Ground

Becoming a good listener includes being open to the communication process, actively listening, having a genuine interest in the other person's point of view and/or opinion, being aware of body language, and treating others with respect. It often includes the ability to find common ground. This means trying to see and understand the viewpoints of others, even if they differ from your own, and working to identify some similarity of interest (common ground.) All too often a barrier to communication is the desire to prove yourself right—not identifying common ground and not listening to others, which leads to miscommunication and possibly conflict.

Example: Finding Common Ground

Chris is the president of the Student Government Association and wants approval from the Dean of Students to spend gift money the university recently received from a donor to "develop a service-learning program on campus." Chris would like to send two student leaders to a conference regarding service-learning programs.

Dr. Smith, the Dean of Students, believes the money would be better spent implementing a comprehensive service-learning program that would impact many students immediately as opposed to just the two attending the conference.

Both Chris and Dr. Smith have a good idea on the development of a new service-learning program yet they differ in the specifics of how to best use the money to reach the goal. If they both tried to prove to the other that their idea is the right or best one, it could lead to conflict. On the other hand, discussing the situation calmly and with respect, trying to really listen and understand the other's viewpoint, and finding common ground could lead to compromise.

How might they find common ground?

Both have the new service-learning program as central to their point of view and both are looking out for the best interest of students. Recognizing this may work to enhance the possibility of a compromise.

ASSERTIVE COMMUNICATION

People have different styles of communication behavior: passive, aggressive, passive-aggressive, and assertive.

Passive

A passive person may be perceived as shy and overly easy going. Often to avoid conflict, they seem willing to go along with the opinions and desires of others. They might be heard saying "You decide, it's okay with me." Ultimately, they may come to resent not being heard and begin to feel like others are taking advantage of their good nature. This can lead to anger, which ultimately may negatively impact a relationship.

Aggressive

The aggressive person wants to win. He or she may be perceived as bossy, controlling, and/or intolerant. This person often forces things to go his or her way leaving others feeling resentful. This can also lead to feelings of alienation, which may cause others to avoid the aggressive person.

Passive-Aggressive

This person may initially appear to be passive and agreeable, but ultimately he or she complains about the decision, usually behind the other person's back. Rarely does the passive-aggressive person confront another directly but will instead complain and vent to others.

Assertive

It is best for students to express themselves in a clear, calm, and respectful fashion. This would be considered assertive communication. When communicating assertively, it is best to articulate the problem or concern clearly without labels or judgments attached; share feelings about the situation or behavior; followed by making a request regarding possible outcomes or changes in behavior.

PROFESSIONAL COMMUNICATION

It is important to develop a rapport with professors and academic advisors. Relationships built with other students, faculty, and advisors can lead to opportunities while in college and beyond. Building professional relationships can be done by utilizing an assertive and respectful communication style. Students are encouraged to begin to develop a professional relationship with their professors. This can be accomplished by attending each class, actively participating in the discussion, and being open minded about course content and various perspectives that might be discussed. When questions arise regarding the course or course content, it is imperative to get clarification from the professor. Going to a professor's office hours offers the opportunity to clarify course expectations, share any student concerns, and interact informally with the professor outside of the classroom, all of which shows interest and are the foundation to building a professional and perhaps even a mentor relationship.

Netiquette

Email is a common means of communication between students and professors. Yet similar to other nonverbal communication, the nuances of voice tone, facial expression, and inflection are often lost, which can lead to misunderstanding the message. Students need to be mindful of this when emailing professors and follow some basic guidelines such as:

- Begin with a proper formal greeting such as Dear Dr. Smith or Hello Professor Smith.
- If it is a large class, it is a good idea to start by stating your name and which class you are in. This is Brandon Jones from your Bio 3 class on Tuesday.
- Use proper spelling and grammar. Do not use abbreviations, slang, and/or emoticons. U R a great prof
- Take time to proofread the message.
- Keep the message concise and to the point.
- Close with Thank you.

Example of Different Communication Styles

A group of friends had made plans over a week ago to go out on Saturday evening to celebrate Homecoming weekend. On Saturday afternoon one of the girls, Nalini, tells the others that she can't make it because she has been asked on a date (by someone she has been interested in for sometime).

Jill (passive response): "That's okay. Have fun." Inside she's feeling resentful that her friend isn't coming at the last minute but doesn't say anything.

Jennifer (aggressive response): "Oh great . . . thanks for giving us such advanced notice. This really makes me angry. I'm not including you in any other future plans." Jennifer is intolerant of the situation and may be trying to control the situation by alluding to the fact that Nalini won't be included in the future, thus impacting their friendship.

Emily (passive-aggressive response); "It's okay . . . I know you've been hoping for this date for a long time." Emily proceeds to complain to her other friends saying, "I can't believe Nalini dumped us at the last minute. It's so rude. I don't care how long she's been waiting for this to happen."

Tonya (assertive response): "I know you had been hoping for this to happen for sometime, but we did have plans (state the problem clearly.) When you change plans at the last minute, I feel like we are not as important to you (state feelings regarding the situation). Is there any way you could reschedule with your date? (make a request and be willing to compromise.)

CONFLICT RESOLUTION

Even when utilizing the best practices as outlined in this chapter related to communication, occasionally conflicts will arise. In fact, conflict is a natural part of life and human interaction. It can be caused by miscommunication, misunderstandings, and differing opinions, beliefs, and values, which can bring about strong feeling and/or emotions. People have different responses to conflict. Some prefer to avoid conflict entirely; others will give in, often believing that by accommodating others the conflict will dissipate, and some seek to deal with the conflict directly with the goal of coming to some type of compromise or solution.

To resolve a conflict it is important to:

1. Begin by defining what exactly the conflict is about. Focus on the conflict not the person. If a conflict arises between two roommates over the cleanliness of their shared space, it is important to define the conflict as room cleanliness and not make it personal (e.g., Try "I'd like to discuss working together to keep our room clean" as opposed to "You are a slob!") It is also important to focus on the pressing conflict and not bring up other things from the past. For example, mentioning that other roommates from prior years said the person was sloppy will not help in the resolution of this conflict.

2. Use "I" statements to communicate feelings as opposed to "you" statements. "I" statements are actually a three-part statement where emotion, behavior, and reason are shared. For example, I feel *embarrassed* (feeling) when I come back to our room after class and *your things are on the floor* (behavior) because I sometimes *like to have friends come back with me* (reason) to study.

Exercise Using the Three-Part "I" Statement

Consider a recent conflict that didn't work out well and try to reframe a response using "I" statements:

I feel _____ (insert feeling)

When you _____ (insert behavior)

because_____ (insert reason).

---

3. Avoid overgeneralizations such as "always" and "never." Statements such as "you *always* leave your things on the floor" or "you *never* clean up after yourself" can cause feelings of defensiveness.

4. Take time to listen attentively to the other person's point of view or concern. It is important not to interrupt or get defensive. Stay calm and respectful. Perhaps the roommate got the impression that a little mess wasn't something terrible or bothersome or he or she had been particularly busy and didn't have time to pick up. Alternatively, she may have been brought up with strict rules requiring keeping her room very clean at home, and now with newfound freedom she is enjoying not having to follow those rules. Most often one roommate is

unaware that the behavior is annoying the other. This type of misunderstanding is common between roommates if they haven't clearly outlined their expectations prior to a conflict.

5. Hopefully both parties are willing to compromise and identify some possible solutions.

6. It is also important to take responsibility for one's behavior, and if something occurred that was wrong or hurt someone else's feelings, an apology is warranted. There is nothing negative about admitting when one is wrong. An apology can sometimes help to build trust and rapport between people and at times can serve to diffuse anger.

OBSTACLES TO EFFECTIVE COMMUNICATION

Although communication is the underpinning of developing and building relationships, some people continue to be faced with common obstacles including:

© R. Gino Santa Maria, 2013. Used under license from Shutterstock, Inc.

- Poor listening skills
- The inability to clarify the meaning of the message
- The need to always be right
- Assuming the other person knows and understands what you mean.

With attention, awareness, and practice, one can improve their communication skills and break down the barriers/obstacles they may face.

DEVELOPING HEALTHY RELATIONSHIPS

Overall, relationships are built on trust and respect for others, the need to set healthy boundaries, and the understanding of expectations of all involved. One of the best parts about college is the opportunity to interact with diverse members of the campus community. Being welcoming and celebrating diversity can open one up to new experiences and new friends.

Roommates

Many students enter college with high expectations of developing a warm and positive relationship with their roommate. Some expect to become "best friends" and while this does occur, in some cases it does not. In fact, more than being best friends, one needs a roommate to be compatible as it relates to living space (cleanliness) and environment (quite study time, guests). Friendship may grow from there.

To truly articulate one's expectations of a roommate requires open and honest communication. Many colleges provide specific forms that guide roommates in designing a "contract" where expectations can be shared and agreement can be reached regarding such things as room cleanliness, times when the room will be quiet for study, overnight and late night guests, sharing and borrowing as it relates to clothes and food, and often a cleaning schedule for the common areas. When speaking with a roommate, "honesty is the best policy." For example, if one roommate is not comfortable having overnight guests every weekend, it should be discussed. Some students come to college believing that they need to be nonchalant about allowing overnight guests but this is not the case. If it makes an uncomfortable situation between roommates, it should be part of the conversation and perhaps a compromise can be reached (e.g., perhaps overnight guests may be allowed only when the roommate who is uncomfortable has plans to be away). If it is not discussed, the relationship has the potential of deteriorating as the semester goes on because one or both roommates will resent the guest situation. Compromises can be made if all roommates have a clear understanding of the initial expectations and agreement.

Along with discussing clear expectations is the need to respect each other's privacy, beliefs, and boundaries. Sharing a room in a residence hall may involve a smaller amount of space than a student is used to at home. For many entering students, this may be the first time they are sharing a bedroom. What initially seems like a fun, ongoing slumber party may wear thin if boundaries such as personal space needs and how much time is spent together, as well as the need for privacy of self and belongings is not discussed early on.

Students need to take some time to get to know their roommate and communicate promptly and often. If something is bothering them, it is best to use assertive communication skills. This is not the time to be passive or passive-aggressive. It is never recommended to let things go in the hope that it will just go away or get better. If the other person doesn't know that playing loud music is disturbing your studying, why would he change his behavior? Too often, when things are left undiscussed, they tend to build up; then when something relatively small occurs, there is a "blow up," which may seem unwarranted to one roommate but the last straw to the other. If after talking to a roommate and trying to work things out through compromise, things are not better, it is advisable to seek assistance from the Residential Life staff.

Romantic Relationships

Romantic relationships often develop and progress during the collegiate years. For many this is an opportunity to meet new people who share similar interests (e.g., major, clubs, or organizations). It is recommended to move slowly and let the relationship grow. There is no reason to rush. In the beginning things may seem very exciting and new. Often because of the proximity, couples can spend a significant amount of time together, yet it is important to take time to explore each other's interests, to look beyond initial attraction to really see one's partners inner qualities, and probably most important is to discuss individual expectations. This requires open, honest communication about boundaries (how much time you will spend together), and exclusivity. If these things are not discussed, miscommunication can occur. For example, if two people are "dating," does that automatically mean it is exclusive? All too often one partner thinks it does while the other does not. Boundaries are also important to discuss. How much time will be spent together? Some enter a relationship and seem to drop their friends and spend every available moment with their new partner. Others want to nurture the new relationship but not at the expense of their friends and family. If one finds that he or she is uncomfortable with any aspect of the relationship, it needs to be discussed. To do so requires mutual respect and trust. If a person finds him- or herself in an unhealthy relationship, it is advisable to seek help from university personnel.

Examples of Healthy and Unhealthy Relationships

EXAMPLES OF HEALTHY RELATIONSHIPS	EXAMPLES OF UNHEALTHY RELATIONSHIPS
Both partners treat each other with respect	One partner tries to control the other
Together, the couple is able to resolve conflict	The couple does not make time to spend together
The couple supports each other	One or both partners use excessive criticism
The couple trusts each other	The couple exhibits poor communication skills
Each partner encourages other friendships	One partner discourages other friendships

Breaking up   Just like the song states, "breaking up is hard to do," but often occurs. If one finds that they are no longer interested in continuing the relationship with their partner, it may be time to break it off. Once the decision is made, it is best to identify a time where the two can meet face to face if possible. (In General: Breaking up should not be done through email, text, or social media.) With the intent of not hurting the other person, one's decision should be shared in a calm and clear manner without anger and when not influenced by alcohol. Utilize "I" statements as opposed to "you" statements; listen to your partner's response.

Sometimes after a breakup, one or both partners want to remain friends. Although this may sound wonderful in theory, often in reality it is difficult to "just be friends." Sometimes this is used as a "nice" way of helping someone deal with the breakup, but statements such as "We can still be friends" should only be used if one genuinely means it. If the breakup is amicable and both parties agree it may be possible to be friends but if one partner still has feelings for the other, it may be quite difficult and painful. In such cases, developing a friendship may be hindered by the hope of rekindling the past romantic relationship. If both partners are committed to the friendship and are willing to have open and honest dialogue about their feelings and can honestly and sincerely see their partner with someone else, it may work.

After a breakup, it is important to deal with any residual feelings of loss, anger, and perhaps depression. It is important to reflect on feelings and to pay extra attention to making healthy decisions. If these feelings persist, students should seek help from the student counseling center.

Family

Relationships with family members often change when a student goes to college. Every family is different, yet often families have high expectations for their son's or daughter's collegiate experience. This may be intensified and add pressure for the first-generation college student. Family members are often excited, worried, and happy that their student is starting college. They may also be feeling a sense of loss. There is the ominous reality that their son or daughter is growing up, becoming independent, and things will never quite be the same. It is a time of growth and change for all. Most families mean well and want to provide the necessary support for success. With growth comes growing pains; to alleviate some of these, communication again is key. Many families benefit from having an open, honest discussion about things such as being safe on campus; standing up to peer pressure; making healthy decisions regarding alcohol, sex, and drugs; as well as the expectation of the amount and type of regular contact the student will have with their family. Conflicts and misunderstandings can occur if the student believes he will call when he needs something and the family expects a call every day.

When communicating with family, students are encouraged to update them on things going on in daily life. Family members genuinely want to hear what's going on. Keep in mind that in high school, parents knew the people in their son's/daughter's life; now their student is exploring and developing new friendships. Families are still interested and need to be updated about the new friends and experiences.

With increased independence comes the need to take responsibility for oneself and one's actions. When dealing with issues that come up in college, it is always best for the student to make contact with university personnel. Most colleges recognize the fact that the student is 18 and therefore an adult. College faculty and administrators respect the student's handling his or her own issues as opposed to retreating and having a parent call.

Relationships while in college can grow, develop, and change. Building strong and solid relationships may take effort, along with honest and clear communication, but can ultimately lead to new and lifelong friendships and bonds with other members of the campus community.

CHAPTER 9

Health and Wellness; Stress Management

> "Being in control of your life and having realistic expectations about your day-to-day challenges are the keys to stress management, which is perhaps the most important ingredient to living a happy, healthy and rewarding life."
>
> —*Marilu Henner*

College is sometimes described as "the best years of your life," yet at the same time, there are tremendous demands placed on a student that can seem to be overwhelming. This is important to consider because the feeling of being "overwhelmed" or stressed can negatively impact a student's ability to develop healthy relationships, hinder his or her ability to study, and adversely affect academic success. The traditional college student today lives in a hyper-enriched world, which encourages multitasking, unregulated access, and competition. They are bombarded with messages and information by the availability of media and social networking 24/7. They have the added pressure to do well in school in the hopes to grow as individuals, as engaged citizens, and to find a meaningful career. It is therefore not surprising that students often crave down time, a chance to slow down and relax, and the opportunity to create a balance in their lives. This chapter will focus on creating balance, which involves maintaining a healthy lifestyle, understanding and managing stress, and avoiding unhealthy coping mechanisms.

MAINTAINING A HEALTHY LIFESTYLE

By the time students enter college, most know the elements of developing and maintaining a healthy lifestyle, but knowing them and living them are two very different things. For some, college is their first extended period of time away from home where they are responsible for maintaining their own lifestyle, including when and what they eat, what time they go to bed and get up, and whether they choose to exercise. These are important choices because choosing not to maintain a healthy lifestyle can cause a student to feel run down and sluggish. It can also impact self-esteem, confidence, and motivation.

Eating Right

Choosing to maintain a healthy diet is a positive step toward developing a healthy lifestyle. Many college students, particularly those who reside on campus, purchase some type of a meal plan. Meal plans offer a variety of food options, including those that are healthy and some (often when eaten in excess) that are unhealthy. Some students find when they first arrive on campus and can make their own food choices that they tend to choose "comfort" and/or fast food, which are often high in calories, carbohydrates, and sugar. This, along with changes in exercise/activity, can lead to weight gain (aka the dreaded "freshman 15"). Alternatively, making good food choices can support the desire to develop a healthy lifestyle, keep one's mind alert, and maintain one's ideal weight, all leading to a general feeling of wellness.

Enjoying a variety of food including fruits, vegetables, whole grains, protein, and dairy are all recommended by the U.S. Department of Agriculture (USDA). The details of the newest program can be found at ChooseMyPlate.gov and outlines the daily-recommended servings for men, women, and children to maintain a healthy diet.

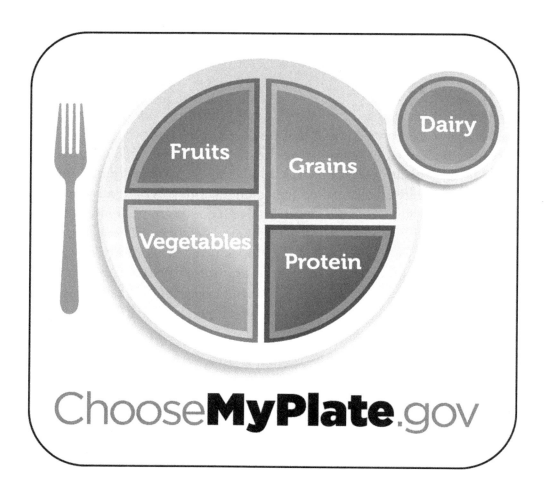

It is also important to read the nutritional labels on the food purchases to avoid any unwanted or "hidden" ingredients. Students should try to limit fried food, sugars, carbohydrates, salt, and caffeine. When they do eat these things, they need to remember to eat them in moderation.

Maintaining One's Ideal Weight

Americans spend millions of dollars on weight-reducing products, diets, and exercise equipment, all with the goal of maintaining their ideal, or losing weight. This is often true of college students who may find that they initially put on a few pounds due to changes in eating and activity as well as stress due to academic and other pressures. Realistically, there is no quick fix to losing weight. The simplest way to lose weight is to decrease caloric intake and increase exercise/activity. For college students it is recommended to avoid fad diets and fasting, which can leave one feeling weak and unable to focus. Further, students would benefit from developing healthy patterns and choices by exercising regularly, eating when they are hungry, and avoiding emotional eating (e.g. eating when lonely or bored).

© paffy, 2013. Used under license from Shutterstock, Inc.

Be aware of disturbances in eating patterns and/or a distortion of body image in oneself or others that can signal disorders including anorexia nervosa, bulimia, binge or emotional eating. Anorexia is when a person drastically curtails food intake to the point where he or she may need to be hospitalized due to lack of nutrition and/or starvation. People who follow this path tend to be perfectionists, have a genuine fear of being fat, and use food as a method of control. Bulimia is a condition involving binging and purging. This is when a person eats to excess on a regular basis and then uses some type of purging behavior (e.g., vomiting, excessive laxatives) to get rid of the food. Binge eating or emotional eating is when a person eats, often to excess, based on their emotions (e.g., bored, lonely, stressed). They do not purge the food, which often leads to weight gain, which can lead to negative feelings, which can lead to emotional eating, thus beginning a vicious cycle. Students who recognize a disordered eating pattern are encouraged to seek professional assistance and support from the health and/or counseling center.

Rest

Not getting enough rest can severely impact a student's ability to do well in school. On average it is recommended that students get 8 hours of sleep per night. This should allow for the student to wake up feeling rested, alert, and energized.

Exercise

Scheduling regular times to exercise not only assists in maintaining one's ideal weight, but it also serves to promote positive feelings. It is recommended that a person include an aerobic activity three to four times per week. Aerobic exercise such as walking, running, biking, swimming, or various machines at a gym provide a workout where one has the opportunity to raise their heart rate for 20 minutes or more. By doing this, the body not only works off calories and

© Warren Goldswain, 2013. Used under license from Shutterstock, Inc.

subsequently excess pounds, but it also allows your brain to release the hormone endorphin, which increases one's feelings of well-being naturally.

Healthy and Supportive Relationships

It is also important for students to establish healthy and supportive relationships both on and off campus. Having a network of positive people available for conversation, social and academic support, and to offer an honest and trusted opinion can provide additional satisfaction and motivation to succeed.

STRESS AND THE COLLEGE STUDENT

The average college student is balancing multiple demands, at a time when he or she is often facing various transitions in life including changes in living environment, developing new relationships, maintaining old ones, and confronting academic challenges.

What Is Stress?

It is important to understand that all stress is not bad. Some stress (called *eustress*) is considered good stress, a level of stress that motivates one to get something done. For example, some students find that a bit of stress before an exam encourages additional study time and organizing study groups. On the other hand, too much stress (or distress) makes the body believe that there is some kind of threat. When the brain perceives a threat, it releases adrenaline, which causes a "flight-or-fight" response. When stress is constant or ongoing, it can become toxic, which is bad for one's health. Too much stress can lead to burnout.

Common Stressors for College Students

Common stressors fall into three main categories: academic, social, and other. Academic stress includes writing papers, taking tests, meeting deadlines, having enough time to study, and competing for grades. College also adds stress in the social context, including taking responsibility for new freedom, living with a roommate(s), relationships, and peer pressure regarding alcohol,

partying, and sex. Other stress includes being separated from your family, choosing a career, and finances—finding a way to afford education.

Stress Assessment

The College Readjustment Rating Scale was adapted from Holmes and Rahe (1967) Life Events Scale to identify the specific stress levels of college students. Please complete the scale on page 75.

Stress Management
College Readjustment Rating Scale

The College Readjustment Rating Scale estimates how stressful life events can affect your health. Each event is assigned a value that represents the amount of adjustment a person has to make as a result of this event.

To determine your stress score, place a '✓' in the box beside the major life events that you have experienced in the past 6 months, or are likely to experience in the next 6 months. Then add up the points that correspond to each of those events.

EVENT	# of Points
☐ death of spouse	100
☐ pregnancy for unwed female	92
☐ death of parent	80
☐ male partner in unwed pregnancy	77
☐ divorce	73
☐ death of a close family member	70
☐ death of a close friend	68
☐ divorce between parents	63
☐ jail term	61
☐ major personal injury or illness	60
☐ flunk out of college	58
☐ marriage	55
☐ fired from job	50
☐ loss of financial support for college (scholarship)	48
☐ failing grade in important or required course	47
☐ sexual difficulties	45
☐ serious argument with significant other	40
☐ academic probation	39
☐ change in major	37
☐ new love interest	36
☐ increased work load in college	31
☐ outstanding personal achievement	29
☐ first term in college	28
☐ serious conflict with instructor	27
☐ lower grades than expected	25
☐ change in colleges (transfer)	24
☐ change in social activities	22
☐ change in sleeping habits	21
☐ change in eating habits	19
☐ minor violations of the law (i.e., traffic ticket)	15
TOTAL SCORE	

Zitzow, Darryl. "The College Adjustment Rating Scale." journal of College Student Personnel (now journal of College Student Development) 25:2 (1984), 160-164. Reprinted with permission of the johns Hopkens University Press.

Interpreting your stress score:
- 149 and below—You have a 1 in 3 chance of a serious health change. Continue to practice relaxation techniques that help you manage your stress.
- 150 to 299—You have about a 50–50 chance of a serious health change within the next two years. Identify your stressors and how they are affecting you physically, mentally, emotionally, and behaviorally. Learn new coping strategies to handle the demands you are facing.
- 300 and higher—You have a high health risk. Consider seeking help from a professional to manage your stress.

Holmes, T.H., & Rahe, R.H. (1967). The Social Readjustment Rating Scale. *Journal of Psychosomatic Research, 11*, 213–218.

Zitzow, D. (1984). The College Adjustment Rating Scale. *Journal of College Student Personnel*, 25(2), 160–164.

INDICATORS OF STRESS

Stress impacts people in various ways. A common indicator is when our bodies respond physically to feeling threatened. Physical signs of stress include a rapid heart rate and breathing, tight muscles, headaches, upset stomach, excessive fatigue, and/or insomnia. Students often report feeling that their heart is racing, they have a feeling of "butterflies" in their stomach, and/or they have cold, sweaty hands.

Stress can also impact a person's emotional state. He or she may become irritable and frustrated, find him- or herself getting angry more often and over minor things, and show signs of anxiety. Students also report that stress impacts them in the classroom by decreasing their ability to concentrate, impacting their memory, and generally feeling exhausted and overwhelmed. These feelings impact their actions in the class and on campus, and they often begin to have negative thoughts such as "I'm going to fail!"

STRESS MANAGEMENT

Stress can affect students' academic success by impacting their ability to do their best in academic and social situations. Unmanaged and prolonged stress can lead to a number of stress-related illnesses such as heart and gastronomical disease, sleep and eating disorders, and/or, depression and anxiety, which is why learning ways to manage stress is so important for students in college as well as into their future.

The first steps in handling stress relate back to the beginning section of this chapter regarding developing an overall healthy lifestyle. It is important for people to take care of themselves by eating a well-balanced diet, scheduling time for regular exercise, and getting enough rest. Following these basic guidelines can help someone stay alert and energized and less likely to feel rundown and get sick. Another part of taking care of oneself involves taking some time for self by participating in activities that are fun and enjoyable, connecting with others who offer support and encouragement, and having a good laugh whenever possible and appropriate. Laughter has been shown to have health benefits by offering an emotional and physical release, which can decrease stress. For some students participating in co-curricular activities and being a good friend are understandably important components of their college life, but also mean additional commitments, which in turn can increase stress. It is advisable that students prioritize the activities/events that are most important to them and learn to say "no" to the others.

Being aware of one's attitude, thoughts, and perspective regarding situations may also serve to decrease or increase the impact of stress. When stressful situations occur, a person's thoughts can exacerbate the situation. For example, when a student is preparing for a final exam, and she has a negative attitude and thoughts about the exam such as "I'm going to fail," it may increase her stress level. It is therefore important to recognize and dispute negative and/or irrational thoughts one might be having and replace them with more positive rational messages.

EXAMPLE

Stressful Situation: You have always been a good student, but after your first semester of college you find yourself on academic probation.

Irrational (Negative) Response: "I'm not smart enough to graduate from college."

Rational (Positive) Response: "I've always been a good student and I still am. I need to work on my time management and study skills. I'll speak to my advisor and if needed get tutors. I can do this!"

EXERCISE

Please identify a stressful situation you have experienced and fill in possible responses (irrational and rational) below

Stressful Situation:

_____

_____

Irrational (Negative) Response: _____

_____

Rational (Positive) Response: _____

_____

When stress does occur, as it invariable does, it is helpful to have learned and practiced relaxation techniques such as deep breathing, visualization, yoga, and progressive muscle relaxation. Students are advised to find one technique that works well for them and continue to practice it. Some schools offer classes and seminars/workshops in stress management, including relaxation techniques. An example of a technique that can be practiced and easily implemented when one finds oneself in a stressful situation is deep breathing (example on page 78.) It can easily be done prior to an exam or a presentation and serves to slow heart rate and breathing, decreases the feelings and tension related to stress, and can help to increase concentration.

DEEP BREATHING EXERSICE

1. Find a quiet and comfortable place to sit.

2. Close your eyes.

3. Take a long slow breath through your nose while counting to 8 or 10. (Your chest should rise and your stomach should extend.)

4. Slowly exhale through your mouth counting to 8 or 10.

5. Repeat three to five times.

If a student finds that stress is impacting or impairing his or her ability to continue with events and activities of daily life, he or she should seek professional assistance such as the college counseling center.

UNHEALTHY WAYS OF COPING

Unfortunately, when faced with stressful situations, some students choose to employ unhealthy coping strategies including turning to alcohol, drugs, cigarettes, food, and caffeine. Often these substances are used to forget one's concerns and/or numb feelings of pain and stress. Although they may give a temporary "high" feeling, it does not last and often leads to crashing low along with the fact that all of these substances when used to excess can lead to addiction.

Alcohol, for example, continues to be quite popular on college campuses. It is often integrated in the social scene for many students, but alcohol slows one's reaction, decreases inhibitions, and impairs judgment, leading to unnecessary arguments/fight, vandalism, and unwanted or unsafe sexual activity. It also impacts academic success as one-third of college students report having missed a class due to alcohol.

Illegal drugs such as marijuana, cocaine, and club drugs are also used by some students to cope with stress, but any relief provided by these substances is only temporary. The stress that comes with acquiring and using illegal drugs may actually serve to compound the stress.

Some students find that when they are stressed, they stop eating or overeat. Many find comfort in food, usually high in carbohydrates and sugars, that make them feel better temporarily. Perhaps it brings back fond memories of home or of an experience, but when food is used as comfort, it is often eaten in excess and often too late at night, causing issues regarding weight, confidence, and self-esteem.

Even though the health risks regarding smoking have been well documented, some students turn to cigarettes to relieve stress. Some come to college having smoked for many years during high school while others begin in college, often blaming stress as the precursor to begin. Like many addictions, once started it becomes habit forming and much more difficult to stop, although many colleges do provide smoking cessation programs and services.

Another common substance overused in college is caffeine. Moderate amounts of caffeine for most people can serve to increase alertness, but excessive amounts lead to nervousness, irritability, headaches, and insomnia. Overuse of caffeine usually begins slowly when a student's sleep schedule is disrupted and he or she feels the need for something to help stay awake in class, but all too often this becomes a daily pattern to stay awake and alert, and at the same time more caffeine is needed. Students also need to be aware that caffeine is not just in coffee. It can be found in energy drinks, chocolate, some teas, and sodas. Serving size is also a concern. A person may believe that he or she is cutting back to one cup of coffee, but if it is a 24 oz. drink, it is the equivalent of four cups of coffee.

CHAPTER 10

Financial Literacy and Money Management

> *"I'd compare college tuition to paying for a personal trainer at an athletic club. We professors play the roles of trainers, giving people access to the equipment (books, labs, our expertise) and after that, it is our job to be demanding."*
>
> —*Randy Pausch,*
> *The Last Lecture*

Attending college can be an expensive proposition, yet many agree that it is an investment in one's future. Trudy Steinfeld (2012) wrote "National economic and labor force data consistently affirm that those with a college education earn more than those without it, and that the more higher education attained means even more lifetime earnings." The decision to attend, and the benefits of earning a bachelor's degree or more, seem evident, but figuring out how to pay for a college education can be stressful for students and their families. This chapter will review the various ways to finance higher education, as well as develop a financial strategy and ways to create and live within a budget.

FINANCING HIGHER EDUCATION

There are multiple ways to pay for a higher education. The most common include loans, scholarship, grants, work-study, and special programs. When considered together, these make up a financial aid package. Before considering how one will pay for college, it is important to identify specifically what amount is to be paid. To do this, the tuition discount rate needs to be identified.

Tuition Discounting

Although tuition discounting may sound somewhat sketchy, it actually is a method to attract, enroll, and retain qualified students who might not be able to pay the full cost of tuition, room, board, and fees (Baum & Lapovsky, 2006). The discount would be the overall cost to attend the college divided by the institutional grants, scholarships, and awards. For example, if the cost to attend Seirup University is $40,000 and the discount rate is 25%, the actual cost averages $30,000. This is extremely important when reviewing the financial aid package awarded by a university. It is also important to note that not everyone automatically receives the discount—it's an average, meaning some may receive more and some receive less.

Scholarships and Grants

These may be awarded to a student based upon financial need or non-need-based awards that are awarded due to some type of merit such as academic achievement, a specific talent, or a special skill or ability (e.g., music, athletics, performing arts). To be eligible for a need-based award, the student most often is required to complete a free application for student financial aid form (FASFA). The college reviews the FASFA and a decision is made regarding the student's possible need. For non-need or merit scholarships and grants, colleges and universities may evaluate a student's academic record, athletic ability, portfolio, or hold auditions. Grants may also be awarded by a college to a targeted population such as women majoring in engineering, students with a disability, or nontraditional students.

The best part about scholarships and grants is that once awarded, there is usually no obligation to pay back the money. On the other hand, there is often some stipulation included in receiving the money such as maintaining a certain GPA or agreeing to participate in intercollegiate athletics or a university performing arts group. Students may receive scholarships and grants from their college, community organizations, and foundations, as well as the federal and state government. There are also numerous websites available for students to research and apply for scholarships and grants.

Loans

Even with planning and being awarded some scholarships and grants, many students find that they are still a bit short and need to take out loans to pay for college. There are also many different types of loans. Usually, the loans offered by the federal government have lower and fixed interest rates. They may be subsidized or unsubsidized. A subsidized loan means that the federal government is covering the cost of the interest on the loan while the student is in school (therefore no interest is accruing), while an unsubsidized loan means that the student is accruing interest while in school, which will be added to the amount needed to repay upon leaving college. Some loans are need based, and a FAFSA form is required to be completed and reviewed for eligibility.

Private loans through banks or other institutions are also available but often have higher and variable interest rates, require a credit check and someone to co-sign the loan; often payments begin right away and are not deferred until the student leaves college. Students are also encouraged to check with their specific office of financial aid to inquire about the availability of low interest loans offered through their college or university. Although loans can be instrumental in helping a student pay for his or her college education, the funds from a loan need to be repaid to the funding provider with interest. There are some loan forgiveness programs often based on the type of work one enters, but overall, when taking out a loan, students should expect that they will pay it back. This is important to keep in mind and not overextend oneself financially.

Work-Study

An overall financial aid package often includes work-study eligibility. Work-study is a federal program where colleges receive money from the federal government to pay students for certain jobs on campus. Often there is a limit on the number of hours a student can work and a set pay scale. The important thing to keep in mind is that work-study is often included in the financial aid package, but rarely does it go directly to pay the tuition bill. Many students find that working on campus provides them with some spending money and may alleviate the need to dip into their savings or request money from family.

© Stephanie Zieber, 2013. Used under license from Shutterstock, Inc.

DEVELOPING A FINANCIAL STRATEGY

Available financial resources may influence a student's academic life by impacting the number of credits the student takes, where the student lives, and the number of hours he or she works. All of these factors may impact a student's academic success. Money (or the lack thereof) can cause students and their families additional stress. Having an understanding of the impact and perhaps one's relationship with money, developing a financial strategy, and learning how to live within a budget can be helpful.

Developing a Financial Strategy Exercise

Consider and respond to the following questions.

1. Are you aware how much money you have in your wallet right now?

2. Are you aware of how much money you typically spend in a day, week, month?

3. Is money important to you today and in the future?

4. Have you ever created a budget? Were you able to live with in it?

The first step in developing a financial strategy includes setting one's financial goals and priorities. For most students, their financial goal and priority while in college is to be able to graduate in four years with as little debt as possible. This is an admirable goal; developing strategies to reach that goal includes being aware and keeping track of one's money and developing and sticking to a budget.

Develop a Budget

Some people hear the word budget and visions of restriction, austerity, and limitations come to mind. Yet developing and living with a budget offers the opportunity to plan, make choices, and finalize decisions. The steps to create and live with a budget are as follows:

1. Identify short- and long-term financial goals, such as paying for college, an opportunity for studying abroad, living on campus, buying a car.
2. Identify income: From a summer job, working during the semester, gifts from family, allowance.
3. Identify expenses: Tuition, room, board, books, transportation, clothes, snacks, entertainment, phone, miscellaneous.

Budget: Academic Year

Goals:

1. Pay tuition, room, and board

2. Save money for study abroad

3. Save money for car

4. Have some fun

5. Don't ask parents for additional money

Income	Amount	Expenses	Amount
Scholarship	25,000	Tuition	34,000
Became a resident assistant	4,000	Room	4,000
Money earned from summer job	6,000	Board	2,000
Parents' contribution annually to college	12,000	Books	1000
Working 15 hours a week on campus *	1,800	Transportation	900
		Clothes	600
		Snacks/Food	1200
		Entertainment	900

Income	Amount	Expenses	Amount
		Phone	1200
		Miscellaneous	600
Total Income	48,800	Total Expenses	46,400

Keep in mind that hours worked is an estimate. Yet this budget would result in $2,400 of income after adjusting for expenses that could be saved to meet the long-term goal of studying abroad and/or buying a car. Some may also find it useful to remove the tuition room and board and create a monthly budget of living expenses.

Annual Budget with Living Expenses (without the academic income and expenses)

Income	Amount	Expenses	Amount
Money earned summer job	6,000	Transportation	900
Working 15 hours a week on campus*	1,800	Clothes	600
		Snacks/Food	1200
		Entertainment	900
		Phone	1200
		Miscellaneous	600
Total Income	7,800	Total Expenses	5,400

Monthly Budget of Living Expenses

Income	Amount	Expenses	Amount
Monthly income of money earned summer job 6000 ÷ 12 = 500	500	Transportation— includes gas, and/or bus, or train fare	75
Working 15 hours a week on campus* 1800 ÷ 12 = 150	150	Clothes	50
		Snacks/Food	100
		Entertainment	75
		Phone	100
		Miscellaneous	50
Total Monthly Income	650	Total Expenses	450

Exercise: Please complete the attached budget spreadsheet (based upon your monthly income and expenses).

Income	Amount	Expenses	Amount
Monthly income		Transportation—includes gas, and/or bus, or train fare	
Working		Clothes	
Other income		Snacks/Food	
		Entertainment	
		Phone	
		Miscellaneous	
		Other expenses	
Total Monthly Income		Total Monthly Expenses	

Developing a budget is an initial step, but more important is living within the budget. Choices often need to be made on purchases and specifically how one spends money. Planning ahead for larger purchases is also important. This is particularly significant if a long-term goal is to save money for a particular item or project. Saving money is often put "on the back burner" for college students, yet with budgeting and planning it can be done. The simplest rule is that to save one must spend less than one makes. There are some saving strategies that can begin in school that can be helpful at all stages of life.

Saving Strategies

1. Buy what you need and avoid impulse purchases. This can often be accomplished by creating a list prior to shopping and sticking to the list.
2. Review your monthly bills, check for accuracy, and pay on time. Paying the minimum amount identified on a credit card bill avoids late fees but serves to accrue and raise the total amount due.
3. Limit your number of credit cards.
4. Make and bring your own lunch when possible. Although buying lunch at school or at work may be convenient, the prices are often much higher than bringing lunch from home.
5. Academic success. Doing well in school equates to not having to take classes over due to poor performance or having to take additional classes to raise a GPA.
6. Share. Whenever possible, consider pooling resources with friends and/or roommates.
7. Identify items that are needed versus wanted. Although one may want a new outfit in the latest style. Consider if is it needed before purchasing.

Credit Cards

Often college students find that they are being enticed to apply for various credit cards. They may find that they "have been preapproved for . . ." xyz gold or platinum credit card. The first thing to consider is need. Is the credit card needed? There are positive and negative sides to getting a credit card. The positive reasons to get a credit card include beginning to develop credit history, which could be advantageous in the future, for the convenience of not having to carry large amounts of cash, and to have a backup in an emergency. The negative aspects of a credit card include the fact that at times it becomes too easy to spend money (perhaps money that one doesn't have), interest rates charged can be quite high, and if payment is not made in a timely fashion and debt builds up, one's credit rating can be damaged. Before considering applying for, getting, and using a credit card, it is important to do some research and comparative review, paying particular attention to any annual fees charged, late fees, and interest rates on any unpaid balance.

FINANCIAL TROUBLE

If a student finds that he or she is in any kind of financial trouble, including not being able to pay tuition or getting overextended with credit card debt, it is imperative that he or she admits there is a problem and tries to get help. Not addressing or avoiding the problem will not make it go away; rather, it adds to a stressful situation. Most schools have staff in the financial aid office who are able to assist with identifying strategies and alternatives to pay for a student's education.

If a student finds that he is overextended on credit cards, has exceeded a credit limit, and/or are late with paying bills, it is recommended that the student gets professional assistance to consolidate the debt and create a payment plan.

CHAPTER 11

Career Development

HOLLY J. SEIRUP

"If you haven't found it yet, keep looking. Don't settle. As with all matters of the heart, you'll know when you find it. And, like any great relationship, it just gets better and better as the years roll on."

—*Steve Jobs (on Career)*

Choosing a career is an important decision, yet making that decision may seem a bit daunting for a traditional college-age student. Many students feel a great deal of pressure to choose the "right" major leading to a lucrative, challenging, and satisfying career. Some of the pressure comes from those closest to them including family, friends, teachers, and school counselors. Beginning in their junior year of high school when the college search process is underway, students are bombarded with questions of "What's your major going to be?" and "What do you want to do/become?" Sometimes bending to the pressure, students declare a major based upon an interest in a subject in which they excelled in high school, which might preclude them from exploring other options in college.

The Bureau of Labor Statistics (2010) reported that on average American workers change jobs 11 times. Other reports have suggested that workers change careers three to five times in their lifetime. Gone are the days when it was common to be employed by a company for one's entire work life. With these changes in employment and career paths, it would seem unnecessary to put pressure on a student to pick a career at 18 years of age. What is significant for students to know is that earning a degree increases overall lifetime earnings, employability, as well as job satisfaction at higher levels than those with a high school education only (Pascarella & Terenzini, 2005).

Career opportunities today and in the future are changing rapidly. There are jobs today that didn't even exist five to 10 years ago. For example, "green" jobs, nanotechnology,

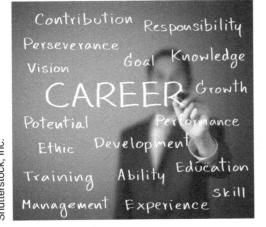

and sustainability studies are currently career options and majors that weren't available in the past. Furthermore, it is expected that there will be new jobs five to 10 years into the future that are currently not available today. The important consideration for students is to continue to develop applicable skills and to be prepared and willing to change as the new career opportunities and jobs develop. This chapter will review elements to consider when choosing a major, which may subsequently impact choosing an initial career, and some general job search strategies.

CHOOSING A MAJOR

Choosing a major may provide structure and focus toward a subject area or knowledge base that a student feels a commitment and/or a passion to study. It can be a step in identifying one's academic purpose and goals. In some departments a major provides membership in a community with other students and faculty with similar interests. Alternatively, a large number of students enter college undecided regarding their major. In fact, at some schools the "undecided" major has the largest number of students. For some being undecided has a negative implication, yet often this means a student has many interests and just can't or doesn't want to make a commitment to study just one. Being undecided also gives students an opportunity to explore areas of interest, various subjects, and possible careers. Also, don't discount the liberal arts; many employers hire people who can communicate effectively (orally and in writing), think critically, and solve problems—many skills stressed in liberal arts courses. Often companies believe that with those very important skills, new hires can be trained in the specific skills required for the job.

Most colleges usually have a deadline where a student needs to declare a major. If, after taking time to explore various possibilities, one is still unsure of a major, it is recommended that the student meet with an academic advisor, faculty, and/or a career counselor to honestly assess interests, talents, and skills. Students may also decide to apply for internships in a particular field as a way of trying a job out. Internships can provide direct insight into a job, which may serve to excite and encourage a student to continue to pursue that career. On the other hand, the intern may find that the actual job is not what he initially expected, and he may choose to consider other options. Keep in mind that sometimes learning what you don't want to do is as important to learning what you do want to do. If after thought, review, and consideration, a student is still having difficulty choosing a major, she may want to consider interdisciplinary majors, or pursuing a double major, minors, and/or certifications. Whenever possible, students should choose to study an area or subject that they enjoy, find challenging, and are passionate about.

Values, Interests, Abilities, and Skills

Students often find that they are much happier and satisfied when their major (and ultimately their career) is in line with their values, interest, abilities, and skills. *Values* relate to the factors in life that one believes have importance or worth. For example, if you feel strongly about the environment, you may find great satisfaction in studying sustainability. If you value work-life balance, you may not be satisfied with a career that involves being on call 24/7. *Interests* include the activities one is involved in and/or subjects studied for which there is a proven level of commitment. Clearly studying and participating in these areas as a major or as a career will increase satisfaction. *Abilities* include individual talents such as being able to sing or play an instrument. Being able to study or work in an area where you have and enjoy a talent can add to satisfaction. *Skills* include the capabilities that are learned and developed over time. Identifying your individual values, interests, abilities, and skills will allow for honest assessment of strengths and weaknesses and the understanding of what factors are truly important to you, which can impact satisfaction with your major and ultimately your career.

EXPLORING CAREERS

If a student feels lost or overwhelmed when thinking about possible careers, it is recommended that he or she begins the exploration process at the college career center. Trained career counselors can assist students in their investigation by administering career assessments such as the Self Directed Search (SDS) or the Myers-Briggs Type Inventory (MBTI). Career assessments can help identify a student's values, interests, abilities, and skills as well as individual personality type, which may impact career satisfaction.

Conducting informational interviews, job shadowing, volunteer opportunities and internships can provide students with valuable approaches in the career exploration process. Each of these provides opportunities to learn more about a particular job prior to making a longer-term commitment. An informational interview may be very beneficial if you have some interest in a career but have never spoken to anyone in the actual job. For example, if you have an interest in music and a talent for playing the cello, but no idea what life is like as a career concert cellist, an informational interview with someone who is or was a concert cellist could

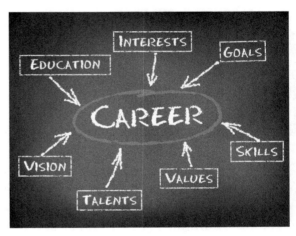

© Vaju Ariel, 2013. Used under license from Shutterstock, Inc.

provide practical information. Students may also find it advantageous to do some research on various careers, attend career fairs and networking events both on and off campus, and become active in related professional organizations.

BUILDING A PORTFOLIO/EXPERIENCE

A common dilemma students face when initially applying for jobs after graduating from college is that employers want to hire applicants who have experience, but they are not willing to hire recent graduates which would give them the opportunity to get the experience. Students can gain the necessary work experience and transferable skill needed for a job by actively and intentionally seeking out opportunities, which will be considered by an employer as related work experience. Examples of this type of experience include:

- Internships: These may be paid or unpaid but often provide student with valuable work related experience and knowledge.
- Research: Doing individual research or working with a faculty member can enhance research skills and may serve to develop a mentor relationship with the faculty member.

- Study abroad: This experience can provide the student with a global perspective that is valued in today's workforce and economy.
- Volunteer/Service Learning: Volunteering may provide transferrable skills that can be related to a job. It may also allow students to highlight their motivation and ability to take initiative.
- Part-Time Job: Working shows that a student has been exposed to some of the "soft" skills of having a job such as punctuality, the ability to effectively respond to feedback, and being a team player.

JOB SEARCH STRATEGIES

The Resume

A resume is an important document that provides an opportunity for a student to put his or her "best foot forward" to potential employers. It serves to consolidate experiences, educational background, awards, honors, and activities into a clear and concise one- or two-page record of accomplishments.

There are a number of methods of formatting a resume. In this section, two will be highlighted: chronological and functional. The *chronological* format is used most often and could be considered the traditional method. It lists education, work, and experiences in chronological order. Anyone reviewing the resume would have a good understanding of the various jobs held and experiences a person may have had.

The *functional* resume is most often used to emphasize various skill sets such as leadership experience or sales expertise as opposed to emphasizing one's employment record. This format is often used by people who have gaps in their resume that they choose not to draw attention to, such as leaving the work force for an extended period of time (due to illness or needing to care for a child or elderly relative.)

Most college students utilize the chronological resume format. The typical resume format includes:

- Contact Information: Include name, address, phone number, and e-mail address. Note: e-mail addresses used on your resume should be professional in nature such as Jsmith@company.com. Trendy and cute e-mail should be avoided such as dancingqueen@company.com or puppylover@company.com.
- Education: Listed in chronological order with the most recent being listed first. GPA is optional. If including your GPA would be advantageous (relatively high), list it. If the decision is made to include GPA, it must be listed honestly and accurately. If hired, many companies request final transcripts for personnel records. Discrepancies in items on a resume such as embellishing GPA may adversely impact an offer of employment.

- Work Experience: Should be relevant to the job and focused on accomplishment such as "supervised and trained 8 employees" or "increased productivity by 10 percent." Be specific and use numbers and percentages to accentuate achievements. When writing the resume, use action verbs such as *created, organized, led,* and *supervised* when describing work experience.
- Other Related Experience: May include experiences that provide transferable skills related to the job, such as study abroad opportunities or volunteer activities that require a significant amount of time, expertise, or skill.
- Activities: Consider listing the undertakings of most importance and requiring the most investment of time and energy. There is a difference between being a member of a planning committee and being responsible for the implementation of an event or program.
- Honors earned
- Languages and/or Computer Skills

There is no need to list personal data (height, weight, marital status) or hobbies/interests unless they seem to be very related to the job. For example, listing travel as a hobby is not directly relevant for a teaching position, yet it might be important for a pilot. Overall, resumes should be easy to read with an appealing format. Finally, it is imperative that students proofread their resumes for spelling and grammatical errors.

Sample Resume Format

REALLY GREAT STUDENT
Street/Apartment
Town, State Zipcode
(xxx) xxx-xxxx
rgstudent@company.com

EDUCATION:

Seirup University, Houston TX	May 2013
Bachelor of Arts in Sociology, Minor in French	
GPA 3.7/4.0	
Fantastic High School, Westwood, MA	June 2009
Honors Diploma	

WORK EXPERIENCE:
Include relevant work experience, focused on accomplishments utilizing action verbs.

OTHER RELATED EXPERIENCE:
Experiences providing transferable skills such as study abroad.

ACTIVITIES:
Include leadership positions and relevant activities.

HONORS & AWARDS:

LANGUAGES & COMPUTER SKILLS:

The Cover Letter

A cover letter can be considered the first writing sample for a potential employer and therefore great care and effort should go into crafting it. Whenever possible, the cover letter should be addressed to the person making the hiring decision (name and title). The first paragraph states the reason for the letter by identifying the specific position for which you are applying as well as how you learned about the job (including if referred to the job or company by someone specific).

Example: How to Begin the Cover Letter

Dr. Geri Stone
Superintendent of Schools
Highland School District

Dear Dr. Stone,

Please accept my resume as formal application for the position of teaching assistant in the Highland school district. I learned of the opening in your District through my faculty mentor Professor Jones.

The middle paragraph(s) of the cover letter include why you are interested in the specific position or the organization and what makes you a good candidate (academic background, professional experience, relevant skills). The final paragraph reiterates interest in arranging a meeting and/or interview and closes with a thank you.

Overall, the cover letter is used to further explain why a specific applicant is a good fit for the job/company. To make this association you would highlight skills and experiences related to the job that would benefit the company. Cover letters are professional but may also serve to express an applicant's personality and passion.

Interview Skills

Developing strong interview skills can have an impact on a student in college and well beyond. Before the actual interview, it is important to spend some time preparing. Whenever possible, find

out what type of interview is being conducted (Is it by an individual or a committee? Is it case, direct, or behavioral?), the anticipated length of the interview (an hour or a whole day), and any additional information required by the company prior to the scheduled interview. It is important to research the position and the employer to understand the industry challenges and trends, as well as the company's mission statement and culture. If time permits, it is recommended for students to participate in practice or mock interviews.

On the day of the interview, arrive early to avoid any stress due to transportation delays, dressed professionally. Throughout the interview you need to remember to answer the questions asked and avoid going off on tangents. Candidates should prepare for direct questions and behavioral questions. Direct questions are an attempt to get information about the person and how he or she might fit in the organization. Behavioral questions focus on how a person responds in various situations and are used to predict future job performance in similar situations.

Example Types of Interview Questions

DIRECT	BEHAVIORAL
Tell me about yourself.	Tell me about the biggest challenge you've had and how you handled it.
Why do you want to work for us?	Give an example of a time when you worked on a team and there was a conflict. What did you do?
What are your strengths/weaknesses?	Describe a decision you made that wasn't popular and how you handled implementing it.

Many find it helpful to utilize the STAR method when answering interview questions. STAR includes explaining the overall **S**ituation that occurred, the **T**ask (goals), the **A**ction one took, and most important, the **R**esults. The results part of the response serves to close the loop and leaves the interviewer knowing that when faced with a challenging situation, the applicant understands how to respond and has had some prior success.

Example of STAR Method

Question: Tell me about a challenge you've faced while in college and how you handled it.

Answer:

Situation: One of my biggest challenges in college was learning how to balance my academic workload and co-curricular activities.

Task: For example, last week I had an exam scheduled for my Biology class, and needed to prepare a speech to run for a leadership position in the Student Government Association.

Action: Both were high priority for me so I decided to plan a schedule two weeks before the exam and election giving me ample time to study and prepare my speech. I was very focused and stuck to the schedule I had developed.

Result: In the end, the planning and scheduling worked. I aced the exam and won the election.

Students need to be honest about their skills, accomplishments, and experience during an interview, while at the same time highlighting how those skills, accomplishments, and experience would benefit the company. As the interview comes to a close, often the interviewer will ask: "Do you have any questions for me about the position or the company?" It is recommended that students prepare approximately two to five questions to ask the interviewer at the end of the interview. It shows interest and that the applicant has done research on the position and/or company. After the interview, send a follow-up thank you letter to express continued interest.

UTILIZING AVAILABLE RESOURCES

When planning for a job search, it is essential to rally all available resources, including your academic advisor, faculty, other students, family, and friends. One of the best resources on campus is the career center. They can provide information on careers, internships, graduate school, give feedback on resumes, provide assessment and mock interviews. It is recommended that students make contact with the career center during their first year of college. Some mistakenly wait until their senior year and by doing so miss out on many informational seminars and workshops about career planning and development.

CHAPTER 12

Achieving Academic and Personal Success

"We are what we repeatedly do. Excellence, therefore, is not an act, but a habit."

—*Aristotle*

College is a time full of transition and change—a time of academic and personal growth and development. Students discover that they have increased independence and opportunity, and at the same time, increased personal responsibility and workload. They are bombarded with new experiences, new people, and the need to make choices. In fact, as Sherfield and Moody (2011) write, "Life is a series of choices. Hard choices. Easy choices. Right Choices. Wrong choices" (p.11). Thus it makes sense that the choices students make in college, and their responses/reactions to the outcomes, can impact their likelihood of achieving their goal of academic and personal success. This chapter will highlight the importance of knowing and utilizing available resources, strategies for success, and ways to deal with obstacles when they arise.

AVAILABLE RESOURCES

To reach their goal of achieving academic and personal success, it is important that students know and rally all of their available resources. This includes human capital, campus and community services, and digital resources.

Human capital includes the people on and off campus who serve as resources and are available to provide assistance. Students should do all possible to surround themselves with positive and empathetic people who can provide encouragement, honest and constructive feedback, and support as they strive to reach their goals. This may include the following:

- *Academic advisors* can assist a student in navigating through the ups and downs of academic life. They are trained to be experts in the curriculum, including specific academic requirements and policy. They are often available to help and advocate for students in cases of emergency or when extenuating circumstances arise.

- *Faculty* are a tremendous resource for students both in and out of the classroom. It is recommended that students visit their professors during office hours to ask questions about something course related or perhaps to discuss the faculty member's research and/or future career paths and opportunities.
- *Mentors.* While on campus, it is advisable to seek out a mentor. This could be a member of the faculty, administration, or staff. Try to identify someone who is recognized as a role model and takes an interest in students and their professional and personal aspirations.
- *Family and Friends.* Students' strongest allies, cheering squad, and support systems are often made up of friends and family. Yet sometimes they are far away or not available, which is why it is also important for students to find support and make new friends on campus. For some, reaching out and making friends seems to come naturally, but for others meeting new people can be overwhelming and stressful. A college campus has numerous and varied opportunities to meet new people and make friends, starting in the classroom and residence halls, by becoming active in student activities, and by attending campus-sponsored events. All of these activities serve to bring people together often with a common interest, setting the foundation for new relationships.

Campus and community services are resources such as learning centers; reading, writing, and math labs; tutorial services; career and counseling centers; health and wellness centers; residential life; the library; and Public Safety. Each of these offices provides services to support student success. Occasionally, students avoid or delay reaching out to these departments feeling uncomfortable or embarrassed by acknowledging they need help. Yet the staffs in these areas are trained to provide just that—along with developing programs and services that create a campus environment conducive for student learning and growth.

Digital resources include the online information to assist students. These resources serve to streamline processes, disseminate information, and offer an alternative method to get answers to questions (particularly at times when offices are closed). They may include information such as a university bulletin or newsletter, deadlines and policy regarding course registration and housing, the student handbook, and community standards just to name a few. To stay current on campus events, students can access the student newspaper or the university website. Most official sites are kept current, and many colleges have also developed a smart phone app to provide the most up-to-date information about everything from what food is being served in the dining hall, the bus schedules, as well as academic information, all in the palm of their hand. With all the technology on campus, it is no surprise that many colleges offer technological services, help, and seminars. With so much information online, it may be tempting to hide behind or overuse technology as a form of communication. Keep in mind that digital resources often cannot replace a face-to-face meeting with university personnel to clarify situations, get questions answered, or provide the opportunity for formal and informal conversation.

Finally, colleges and universities provide human capital, campus services, and digital resources in order to create an environment that supports students as they strive to reach their academic and personal goals. These resources are valuable tools for students who are navigating higher education. Providing them is the universiy's responsibility; making full use of them is the students'.

STRATEGIES FOR SUCCESS

One of the most important strategies for success is believing in yourself! This involves knowing and appreciating who you are, including having a realistic outlook of your individual strengths and weaknesses. With this understanding you can make the most of and better utilize your strengths and at the same time begin to work on improving areas of weakness. For example, consider a student who had a strong academic record in high school yet is now struggling in college. Her strength is her proven ability to do well academically. Her weakness, which is negatively impacting the current outcome, is being overextended with activities and work (not being able to balance her time commitments). By identifying her strengths and weaknesses, she can respond by developing and implementing time management skills that could give her the time needed to study and do well academically again (her strength).

Although there is much talk about success and reaching goals, defining what success means to each individual is an important step. Some believe academic success is graduating with honors; others believe it's simply graduating. Consider how you define academic success.

Exercise

Please complete the following sentence.

For me, academic success is:

_____

Once you have a clear understanding of how you define success, measurable and attainable goals can be developed, and you can begin to work toward achieving them. For example, if a student's definition of academic success is graduating in four years with honors (3.5 or above), and he struggles his first semester, earning a 1.9, he will need to set some goals to reach his definition of academic success. He might set a goal of earning a 4.0 the next semester, which in measurable, but without any changes in behavior, is it attainable? It is important to set goals, but you also need to consider how you can reach those goals. In this situation, it may realistically take a few semesters to reach the GPA goal. Many times in these circumstances, a student may need to make some changes and perhaps choose to modify some existing habits and/or to develop new and positive habits such as enhancing or implementing time management and study strategies or cutting back on activities or hours worked in an effort to reach the goal.

Habits are regular patterns of our thoughts, actions, and behavior that we do/have—often subconsciously. They may be positive habits such as going to the gym on a regular basis, creating a study plan, or maintaining a positive outlook on life. On the other hand, negative habits can include smoking, procrastination, leaving work until the last minute, or having a pessimistic outlook on life. We may be aware of our bad habits and may even want to (or have tried to) change them. Yet, changing a habit is not as easy as it sounds. For example, the student who earned a 1.9 GPA may recognize that he has a bad habit of procrastinating and leaving his work until the last minute. In response, he may begin the next semester with a goal of keeping up with all assigned readings and course work but as the semester moves on, he may slip back into his old habits. It often takes hard work and commitment for change to occur. Sometimes people revert to old comfortable habits, but they should not give up. Some say to change a habit takes a minimum of 21 days, but it can be done, and people make positive changes in their life everyday.

Examples of positive changes to achieve academic and personal success include:

- Developing and using positive time management strategies
- Knowing your learning style
- Practicing effective study skills
- Getting involved through networking, volunteering, and student activities
- Making healthy and responsible lifestyle decisions
- Actively listening to others
- Communicating assertively
- Knowing your limits and being kind to yourself
- Using all available resources and seeking help when needed
- Maintaining a positive, optimistic outlook on life

Having a positive attitude and exhibiting motivation and persistence can also impact outcomes and ultimately success. Maintaining a positive attitude and positive thoughts is not always easy, particularly if you are under stress or feeling overwhelmed. When negative thoughts creep into your mind, it is imperative to reframe and replace them with positive ones. Try using positive self-talk, giving yourself positive messages such as "I can do this." Developing a positive attitude can give a student the necessary confidence to grow, take risks, be open to opportunity such as meeting new people, and ultimately overcome setbacks and obstacles.

OBSTACLES

When setbacks occur or obstacles arise (and they will), be aware that there are usually multiple ways to approach them. For example, if a student finds that she has fallen behind with her work, she can choose not to take action. Feeling "stuck," she does nothing and runs the risk of not doing well in the course. Alternatively, she can choose to take action and look at possible alternatives including speaking to her professor, requesting an extension for a late project, rallying her resources, and seeking assistance, perhaps by finding a tutor or peer advisor.

© Leena Robinson, 2013. Used under license from Shutterstock, Inc.

Make the commitment to use the strategies and tools outlined in this text to create lasting and positive habits, identify and rally resources, and take action. Developing a positive attitude, learning to make responsible, healthy decisions, and reaching out to available resources when obstacles arise will lead to success in school, work, and your personal life today and into the future.

© Andresr, 2013. Used under license from Shutterstock, Inc.

BIBLIOGRAPHY

Baum, S., & Lapovsky, L. (2006). *Tuition discounting: Not just a private college practice.* New York: The College Board.

Berg, C., Ling, P., Guo, H., Klah, C., Thomas, J., Ahluwalia, J., & An, L. (2011). Using market research to understand health behaviors among college students. *College Student Journal. 45*(4), 726–737.

Carter, C., Bishop, J., & Kravits, S. (2011). *Keys to effective learning: Study skills and habits for success.* Boston: Pearson Allyn & Bacon.

Choose My Plate (2013). Retrieved on March 5, 2013 from www.choosemyplate.gov

Colbert, B. J. (2009). *Navigating your future: An interactive journey to personal and academic success.* Upper Saddle Brook, NJ: Pearson Prentice Hall.

Darren, G., Dixon, S., Stansal, E., Gelb, S., & Pheri, T. (2008). Time diary and questionnaire assessment factors associated with academic and personal success among university undergraduates. *Journal of American College Health 56*(6), 706–715.

Davis, M., Eshelman, E. R., & McKay, M. (2008). *The relaxation and stress reduction workbook* (6th ed.). Oakland CA: New Harbinger.

Downing, S. (2014). *On course: Strategies for creating success in college and in life* (7th ed.). Boston: Wadsworth.

Dweck, C. (2006). *Mindset: The new psychology of success.* New York: Random House.

Fabricant, F., Miller, J., & Stark, D. (2014). *Creating career success.* Boston: Wadsworth/Cengage.

Ferrett, S. (2011). *Peak performance: Success in college and beyond* (8th ed.). New York: McGraw-Hill.

Gardner, J., & Barefoot, B. O. (2012). *Your college experience: Strategies for success.* Boston: Bedford/St. Martin's.

Gettinger, M., & Seibert, J. K. (2002). Contributions of study skills to academic competence. *School Psychology Review 31*(3), 350–365.

Holmes, T. H. & Rahe, R. H. (1967). The social readjustment rating scale. *Journal of Psychosamatic Research 11*, 160–164.

Kanar, C. C. (2014). *The confident student.* Boston: Wadsworth/Cengage.

Mancinim M. (2005). *Time management.* New York: McGraw Hill.

Moule, J. (2012). *Cultural competence: A primer for educators.* Boston: Wadsworth/Cengage.

National Institute of Mental Health. (2013). Mental Health Information. Retrieved on March 4, 2013, from www.nimh.nih.gov/index.shtml

Pascarella, E. T., & Terenzini, P. T. (2005). *How college affects students: A third decade of research.* San Francisco, CA: Jossey-Bass.

Rose, S., & Seirup, H. (2012). Promoting mindful student behaviors to promote academic success. *Procedia—Social and Behavioral Sciences.* (4th Quarter).

Seirup, H., & Rose, S. (2011). Exploring the effects of hope on GPA and retention among college undergraduate students on academic probation. *Education Research International.* 2011. doi:10.1155/2011/381429.

Sherfield, R. M., & Moody, P. G. (2011). Cornerstones: Creating success through positive change (6th ed.). Boston: Pearson Allyn & Bacon.

Smith, J. (2002). *Stress management: A comprehensive handbook of techniques and strategies.* New York: Springer.

Snyder, C. R., Shorey, H. S., Cheavens, J., Pulves, K. M., Adams III, V. H., & Wiklund, C. (2002) Hope and academic success in college. *Journal of Educational Psychology 94*(4), 820–826.

Steinfeld, T. (2012) [Blog Post] Retrieved from www.forbes.com/sites/trudysteinfeld/2012/12/04/is-college-worth-it

U.S. Bureau of Labor Statistics (2013). Occupational Outlook Handbook. Retrieved February 12, 2013, from www.bls.gov/ooh

U.S. Bureau of Labor Statistics (2012). Occupational Outlook Handbook. Retrieved January10, 2013, from www.bls.gov/ooh

Van Blerkan, D. (2006). *College study skills: Becoming a strategic learner.* Boston: Thompson-Wadsworth.

Your preferred learning style. (2007). How to study.com: A study skills resource site. Retrieved January 12, 2013, from www.howtostudy.com

Zitzow, D. (1984). The college adjustment rating scale. *Journal of College Student Personnel, 25*(2), 160–164.